# CONTENTS

# POP STAR

# Goddesses

# POP
# STAR
# *Goddesses*

And How to Tap Into Their Energies to Invoke Your Best Self

## JENNIFER KEISHIN ARMSTRONG
### Illustrations by Robin Markle

MORROW
GIFT

An Imprint of WILLIAM MORROW

## NOTE ON SOURCING

Quotes from and about the artists were culled from published and recorded interviews and are cited within the text when necessary for clarity and context. More detailed sourcing information is available in Sources.

# INTRODUCTION
# WHAT IT MEANS
# TO BE A POP STAR
# GODDESS

*I have loved Britney Spears* from the first time I heard ". . . Baby One More Time," because it takes a stronger person than I to resist ". . . Baby One More Time." I continued to love her because I shared my Britney worship with my sister, who is ten years my junior and just a little bit younger than Britney herself. But over the two decades of my fandom, Britney has come to mean more to me than earworms and dynamic dance moves. She has helped me to channel my "Work Bitch" spirit. I've always had ambition, but Britney showed me how to take it to another level, how to power through in the worst of times.

Plenty of other stars on my most-played list have also had this effect on me. Kelly Clarkson proved to me that even the most successful among us could be regular, could be goofy and imperfect while also blessed with superhuman talent. And Beyoncé, well . . . what *would* Beyoncé do? I have asked myself this question over and over in my own professional life. Beyoncé would negotiate for more money. Beyoncé would demand a do-over here. Beyoncé would practice this again and again until it's perfect.

Pop Star Goddesses direct my goals every day, and I am grateful to them for this.

Some, like Britney, have also served as what I'd call an "inspirational cautionary tale"—not immune to difficulties, but always, somehow, a survivor. We all know that in 2007, Britney had one of the most iconic public meltdowns of all time. To me, this doesn't disqualify her from goddesshood; in fact, she began her journey toward goddesshood at this time. She shaved her head in full view of cameras at a Los Angeles salon, beat back paparazzi with an umbrella, and was hauled on a stretcher from her home to a hospital. The fact that she survived that period at all remains a miracle. The fact that she has continued to make great music and set trends with a four-year residency in Las Vegas impresses me even more.

Britney has endured public ups and downs to this day. Over the past few years her Instagram has become essential viewing, showing us Britney at her best. There, we've seen her make watercolor paintings, work out with her trainer/model boyfriend, and dance like it's 2002. And on this very same social media platform, she has also shown glimpses of her vulnerabilities. There, she announced the cancellation of her second Las Vegas residency and her decision to take time off to care for her ailing father. In 2019, Britney checked into a mental health treatment facility, which stoked fans' worry anew; she essentially confirmed her decision to get help with an April 2019 post on Instagram that read, "Fall in love with taking care of yourself, mind, body, spirit," and the caption, "We all need to take time for a little me time." But these low moments, documented more publicly than her previous struggles thanks to social media, further prove that her survival instincts continue to do battle with the demons of her life. She gives us all ample cause to root for and draw inspiration from her.

This vulnerability is consistent with the stories of goddesses throughout history. Goddess stories hinge on weaknesses as well as strengths. Goddess worship and culture span time and cultures, from the Greeks and Romans to the Celts, Hindus, and Sumerians. Devotees have called upon these female representations of divinity to draw strength from their special qualities, trials, and triumphs for thousands of years.

These days, we have pop stars, whose outsize personalities can be seen as a kind of goddess energy. A pop star's goddess ability determines her persona as well as her staying power in the public eye. Without goddess-like symbolism, a pop star faces an uphill climb to remain relevant. Musical skill alone won't do it. Narrative keeps fans interested.

We've stuck with Cher, the matriarch of modern Pop Star Goddesses, for decades after her debut because of her goddess energy. And she begat the holy trinity of the 1980s: Madonna, Whitney Houston, and Janet Jackson. These icons turned their unique qualities—some would even say their weaknesses—into strengths.

Cher embraced being "exotic" and svelte at a time when most stars were one of two types of busty white blonde: cute blonde or sexy blonde. She had a low voice and long, dark hair and bold Armenian features. Millions of girls with dark coloring and flat chests worshipped at the altar of Cher, who showed us we were beautiful, too.

Madonna, named for the Virgin Mary, made her rebellion against Catholic repression her stock-in-trade and set the model for the modern Pop Star Goddess in the process. Her opposite, Janet Jackson, shy and quiet offstage, transformed into a precise, dynamic performer when the lights came up; Janet's quiet resolve allowed her to break free from a controlling family full of performers. Whitney Houston represented diva perfection (an image shattered in her later years by the much more complicated—and interesting—woman underneath). In the 1980s, millions of American girls wanted to be Madonna, Janet, Whitney, or some combination of the three.

Thanks to these original four, Pop Star Goddesses have proliferated in the decades since, and Cher, Madonna, and Janet have taken on more dynamic and sophisticated attributes with time. Pop Star Goddesses, after all, age with the rest of us. It turns out this is another of their goddess strengths: they exemplify different approaches to aging. Cher and Madonna have chosen to fight aging with their trademark determination. Janet Jackson had her first baby at fifty. The goddess role models we choose sometimes change as we age. As I've gotten older, Carla Bruni, the cool French chanteuse who also spent some time as the first lady of France, has become one of my favorite Pop Star Goddesses. When you're over thirty-five, you might prefer to evoke some Bruni-like sophistication rather than emulate Rihanna's zero-fucks attitude.

We can all use a little Pop Star Goddess energy in our lives. Luckily, we have a wide variety of goddesses to choose from. *Pop Star Goddesses* explores thirty-five current goddesses for whatever situation you may find yourself in and suggests some ties to ancient goddesses who share qualities with our favorite pop stars of today. You might find that some days you need a shot of Cardi B's rags-to-riches determination; other days you might want to become a Lady Gaga social justice warrior. Each Pop Star Goddess finds strength in her uniqueness, but her qualities are also universally valued: take Janelle Monáe's public embrace of her sexuality, Ariana Grande's ability to evolve, or Alicia Keys's earth-mother wisdom, to name a few. Kelly Clarkson, known for her honesty, will take down a powerful music mogul who's treated her poorly or cop to her love of wine in interviews. British–Sri Lankan rapper M.I.A. will get more

political than anyone is comfortable with and models a gangsta energy unusual for female stars. Nicki Minaj flaunts every inch of her sexuality and brags about her prowess in the bedroom, her business acumen, and her legit rap skills, just as men have done since hip-hop began.

In these pages, you'll find nuggets of wisdom from Pop Star Goddesses, inspiration from their stories, and thoughts from others who have been inspired by these goddesses. Sample a few and see how they harmonize with your own journey.

# ADELE

## Goddess of Wisdom Through Heartbreak

*Adele Adkins*—a teenager from Tottenham, a neighborhood on the outskirts of London—browsed the selection at a record store in the city and found herself drawn to the jazz section. It was 2003, a time when 50 Cent, the Black Eyed Peas, and Nelly dominated the radio. But Adele was more intrigued by Etta James and Ella Fitzgerald. As she listened to these soulful crooners, the teenager had what she would call a musical "awakening," when describing it to the *Telegraph* in 2008.

Five years later, she released her debut album, a modern take on the work of those classic soul singers, called *19*—the age she was when she wrote the songs. "I just kinda remember becoming a bit of a woman during that time," Adele said. "And I think that is definitely documented in the songs." A critical success, *19* hit number 1 in her home country.

Adele has since become an international star with her polished old-school sound, channeling her heartbreak into massive hits like "Someone Like You" and "Hello." She scored her first number 1 in the United States with "Rolling in the Deep," which is about her first major breakup, an experience that she told *Rolling Stone* "made me an adult." The same breakup fueled her next number 1, "Someone Like You."

Both "Rolling in the Deep" and "Someone Like You" appeared on Adele's second album, *21,* one of the great breakup records of all time. She recorded the songs with a live band, and her musical authenticity stood out in a time when most artists relied on electronic sounds and Auto-Tune: "Her singing was so strong and heartbreaking in the studio, it was clear something very special was happening," said one of *21*'s producers, Rick Rubin. "The musicians were inspired, as they rarely get to play with the artist present, much less singing."

Critics and audiences across generations and cultures responded to this method. As Guy Adams wrote for the *Independent* in 2011, "There are two approaches to the business of being noticed by today's record-buying public. The first . . . revolves around oodles of hype and ever-more preposterous wardrobe selections. The second . . . requires . . . the confidence to let your music do the talking." Point taken, even if Guy Adams is clearly shading Pop Star Goddess Lady Gaga here.

Though Adele found initial inspiration in classic performers like James and Fitzgerald, she has openly admired more contemporary pop artists, too. She adores Beyoncé, the Spice Girls, Pink, and Amy Winehouse as much as the rest of us. With the release of her third album, *25,*

Adele became an undeniable music industry fixture in the same class as her pop idols: *25* was the top album of 2015 in the United States. "Adele Is Music's Past, Present, and Future," said a *Time* magazine headline. The industry took note that Adele's polished throwback sound sold millions of actual, physical albums at a time when many consumers streamed individual tracks. Critic Chris Willman wrote for *Billboard* that "what Adele has really revived, more than any style, is the primacy of the album as an emotional experience that a single digital track is not equipped to provide."

However, her mainstream appeal morphed into something less desirable at the 2017 Grammy Awards when *25* beat Beyoncé's masterpiece *Lemonade* for Album of the Year. Adele now represented all that was wrong with the white-centric, stuck-in-the-past awards show. She knew it and said so in her (non-)acceptance speech: "I can't possibly accept this award. I'm very humble and I'm grateful and gracious, but my artist of my life is Beyoncé and the *Lemonade* album was just so monumental—Beyoncé, it was so monumental—and so well-thought-out and so beautiful and soul-baring. All us artists here, we fucking adore you." Her speech didn't come off perfectly; Adele also referred to how *Lemonade* had made her "black friends" feel empowered, a well-intentioned remark that hewed a little too close, for some, to tokenism.

But Adele, too, had expanded representations of women in media; she fought for women's right to exist beyond a

size 6. Designer Karl Lagerfeld called her "a little too fat" in an interview. Fox News's Neil Cavuto ran a segment in 2013 that featured a nutritionist who scolded Adele and Kelly Clarkson for their body types. The nutritionist worried both Pop Star Goddesses' prominent success would send the message to audiences that "I could be overweight like her. I don't need to address these issues in my life."

Adele's standard response to such chatter: "My life is full of drama, and I don't have time to worry about something as petty as what I look like," as she told *Rolling Stone*. Or: "I have insecurities, of course, but I don't hang out with anyone who points them out to me," as she told *Vogue*. Or: "I've never wanted to look like models on the cover of magazines. I represent the majority of women, and I'm very proud of that," as she told *People*.

That sentiment cuts to the heart of her appeal: she seems like she could be any of us—until we hear that magical voice when she sings, and the powerful truths that come with it.

## Adele's Ancient Goddess Sister

# RADHA

Radha is the "goddess of romantic longing," according to Sally Kempton's *Awakening Shakti: The Transformative Power of the Goddesses of Yoga*. Adele has connected with audiences worldwide through her passionate love songs and tapped into the ecstasy, the tumult, the anger, and the acceptance that comes with romantic love. In "Hello," she imagines a call to an old lover to make amends, but in "Someone Like You," she addresses an ex as she hopes to someday find another love as great as the one they shared. In "Send My Love (To Your New Lover)," she hopes her ex will apply lessons learned from their relationship to his new one; in "Water Under the Bridge," she scolds a current lover who underplays their passion. And, of course, "Rolling in the Deep" goes full vindictive kiss-off. All these songs contain shades of Radha.

Like Adele, Radha approaches love with the best of intentions and without deliberate manipulation; she is motivated by love, though that can lead to messiness. Radha adores bad-boy Krishna, who cannot be restricted to just one love by his nature. To be more like Radha or Adele, you must look for the divine spark in your lover and you must stay vulnerable to your own tender feelings, no matter how the object of your affection reacts. For you to achieve your full potential, your heart must remain open, even to welcome heartbreak and its possibilities for growth.

## Invoke Adele for

Being your most mature self
Presenting a polished image
Making the best of a breakup
Loving with reckless abandon
Doing things the old-fashioned way

## How to channel Adele's goddess energy

Enjoy "the classics" in your preferred medium—
books, music, movies, or TV.

Choose a "uniform" for your daily life and work: Adele, for instance,
nearly always wears a black dress onstage, which makes for easy
decisions and a consistent image.

Go all in on a style flourish from the past: a bouffant,
winged eyeliner, red lipstick.

## JOURNAL RIFFS

If you could be a major figure from the past, who would it be and why?

Write a letter (that you don't send) to the person who
broke your heart the most.

If you were to make a record about your current life, what would its
overarching theme be? What would some of the song titles be?

## power songs

"Hello"
"Someone Like You"
"Send My Love (To
Your New Lover)"
"When We Were
Young"

"Set Fire to the Rain"
"Water Under the
Bridge"
"All I Ask"
"Rumour Has It"
"One and Only"

"Remedy"
"Cold Shoulder"
"Rolling in the Deep"
"Hometown Glory"
"Skyfall"
"Chasing Pavements"

# ALICIA KEYS

## Goddess of Quiet Confidence

*Alicia Keys* once had to pay tribute to Prince—in front of Prince.

As she began playing his song "Adore" on the piano onstage at the 2010 BET Awards, she acquitted herself nicely. Dressed in a strapless black top and black pants hugging her pregnant belly, she delivered exactly what anyone would expect, a version of "Adore" in her own classic R&B, piano-driven style. The icon himself—being honored that night with a Lifetime Achievement Award—nodded along appreciatively, casually, from the audience.

Then, about two minutes in, Alicia grabbed the mic and stood up, crawling, panther-like, onto the top of the black grand piano. The mood changed. Maybe a visibly pregnant woman prowling sexily on top of a concert instrument should not have come as such a shock, but it did. A perfectly calibrated shock—not distasteful, just beautiful and right.

Prince, a master of performance if there ever was one, went bug-eyed and grabbed the forearm of the woman sitting next to him. As Keys arched her back and continued to sing, Prince glanced down the row of women seated next to him with a look that said, "Do you *see* this?" As Alicia sang the second verse, with her own slight variation on the lyrics—"They know this is serious / I don't fuck with you for kicks"—Prince applauded and pumped his fist. She had officially blown Prince away.

Alicia Keys had entered the public arena a decade earlier, fully formed, and has only gotten better since. In the beginning, at twenty, she had a mature air common for New York City kids: "I grew up in the middle of everything," she said. "I walked the streets alone, I rode the trains alone, I came home at three in the morning alone, that was what I did." The introductory a cappella vocal run in her 2001 debut single, "Fallin'," left little doubt: this young woman was talented in a way rarely associated with pop stars. She has remained consistent in the twenty years of her career that have followed, always grounded and unfazed by the spotlight, thanks to one factor—her undeniable gifts.

She was born Alicia Augello Cook on January 25, 1981, in New York's Hell's Kitchen, to a paralegal/actress mother and a flight attendant father. Later, Alicia adopted a stage name that reflected her piano skills. She began studying classical piano at seven and graduated from New York City's Professional Performing Arts School as valedictorian. "Classical piano totally helped me to be a better songwriter and a better musician," she said in a 2005 interview. "I knew the fundamentals of music." A&R executive Peter Edge recalled, "I remember that I felt, upon meeting her, that she was completely unique. I had never met a young R&B artist with that level of musicianship."

Her 2001 debut album, *Songs in A Minor*, which included "Fallin'," made her an instant pop star, with both the single and the album topping the *Billboard* charts; she won five Grammys for the record, including Best New Artist and Song of the Year for "Fallin'." Alicia's 2003 follow-up, *The Diary of Alicia Keys*, solidified respect for her with its definitive lack of Auto-Tune or guest features—it was 100 percent, all-natural Alicia at her most personal.

She made an immediate impact, as noted by actress Kerry Washington, who wrote about Alicia for *Time* magazine's 100 Most Influential People list in 2017: "Alicia Keys' debut, *Songs in A Minor*, infused the landscape of hip-hop with a classical sensibility and unfolded the complexity of being young, gifted, female and black for a new generation. Alicia became an avatar for millions of people, always remaining true to herself."

She married producer Swizz Beatz in 2010 and gave birth to their first child together, Egypt Daoud Dean, in October of that year. Two years later, she put out her fifth album, *Girl on Fire*, and the title song became one of her biggest signature hits, a feminist anthem made for feeling like an Olympic-level athlete even as you run your first half marathon or 10K.

Alicia took her position as a public figure and role model seriously, advocating for more natural beauty standards by going makeup-free starting in 2016, at the age of thirty-five—even for magazine shoots and during her stint as a coach on TV's *The Voice*. The cover of that year's album, *Here*, her sixth full-length release, pictures her in black and white with a bare face and natural hair. Other celebrities, such as Gabrielle Union, Adele, Mila Kunis, and Gwyneth Paltrow, followed suit, at least in some photos on Instagram.

Alicia said her no-makeup campaign was her reaction to years of pressure in the entertainment industry. "If we have any hips or any thickness or width with us, we're fat," she said in a *Variety* interview, explaining how she was led to think in the early years of her career. "We torture ourselves; we don't eat. I've experienced all of that. I was subscribing to this sick identity. . . . Stay in your place, be feminine, be a lady, don't make too much noise."

The makeup-free idea began with the writing and recording of *Here*, specifically the track "Girl Can't Be Herself," which includes the lyrics: "Who says I must conceal what I'm made of / Maybe all this Maybelline is covering my self-esteem." She wrote in a piece for Lenny Letter: "I don't want to cover up anymore. Not my face, not my mind, not my soul, not my thoughts, not my dreams, not my struggles, not my emotional growth."

Of course, having flawless skin helped. She even experienced some backlash in the media: the *Guardian* called the makeup-free celebrity trend "the humblebrag movement of the moment." In the inevitable backlash to the backlash, Jezebel weighed in: "Good question: having a face and not smearing cosmetics upon it: is it a political statement, sloth, or, uh, some kind of weird fashion thing? Or could it be some strange, unheard-of fourth option . . . such as being a human in possession of a face who doesn't feel the need to apply products to it, and it is really just not a big deal?"

Alicia developed a focused skin care routine, which she and her team shared in the name of transparency. "Alicia gets regular facials, does acupuncture and she eats healthy and exercises," her beauty specialist, Dotti, told *W* magazine. "She knows you have to invest internally for your skin to look great externally. It's also about how you process your energy." The no-makeup policy changed Dotti's role from applying makeup to keeping Alicia's face looking healthy, including using a jade roller, masks, cucumbers, MV Organic Skincare 9 Oil Cleansing Tonic, and jojoba oil. Alicia also clarified that she wasn't anti-makeup; she would still wear it occasionally and had no qualms with anyone who did.

Alicia's stripped-down aesthetic matched the vibe of *Here,* her first album in four years. She said the long break between records, which included her second pregnancy, resulted in a backlog of inspiration; she said: "The music for this album was created so fast—the fastest I've ever created music before. It was like raining down every night." This output included the single "Blended Family

(What You Do for Love)," an autobiographical homage to her husband and his children from a previous marriage.

Three years after first starting her no-makeup campaign, she was still rocking a bare face as she hosted the noticeably grounded, kind, female-friendly 2019 Grammy Awards. Alicia made her visual statement with several outfit changes: a long red gown with a plunging neckline for the red carpet; a green dress with a head scarf for the opening; a black, wide-brimmed hat, a black leotard top with a deep-V neckline, and sparkly pants for her two-piano performance; a black leather jumpsuit and diamond necklace for the next segment; and a red jumpsuit with a cape for the remaining part of the show. Her presence, meanwhile, made its own impact on an awards show that had been (rightly) criticized the previous several years for racist and sexist selections.

Alicia's hosting gig fit in with her own long-term plan for industry domination—not just for herself, but for all women. She told *Variety* in 2018 that women need to "infiltrate our industries" to take the power due to them. "Does that mean we have to go to war between men and women?" she said. "That's not going to create the change we want to see."

"All women are naturally badass," she said in a 2015 Twitter post. That might be true, but having a role model like Alicia to guide us to the heights of our badassery doesn't hurt.

## Alicia's Ancient Goddess Sister
# SEKHMET

Sekhmet lends us strength beyond our expectations and promises us happy endings if we use our strength well. Alicia has always approached her career and public persona from a place of personal strength—not lingering on what is wrong with the system, but seeking the best ways to make it right, whether she's giving up makeup, hosting the Grammys, or encouraging herself and other women to "infiltrate our industries." She has never underestimated herself, and she doesn't want us to underestimate ourselves, either. When internet trolls criticized her makeup-free appearance and media critics called her no-makeup movement disingenuous, she stuck with it anyway, explaining that she'd chosen the path that made her feel best about herself. Egyptian sun goddess Sekhmet's name means "strong and mighty," according to Doreen Virtue's *Goddess Guidance Oracle Cards*. Sekhmet is often shown with lions, or as a half-lion, half-woman hybrid, echoing the wildcat crawl Alicia has sometimes employed onstage and the fierceness with which she guards her own sense of self and power.

## Invoke Alicia for

Wisdom
Bravery
Inspiring others
Transcending the limits of your title, job, or position

## How to channel Alicia's goddess energy

Give yourself a "stage name" that reflects your most unique
quality as a person or professional.

Listen to and learn about classical music.

Try going makeup-free or find some other way of
embracing natural beauty that works for you.

Adopt more natural beauty products. Brands such as Beautycounter make
it simple, adhering to an all-natural ethos. For more help, check out the
Environmental Working Group's online cosmetics database:
www.ewg.org/skindeep.

## JOURNAL RIFFS

How can you "infiltrate" your industry on behalf
of both yourself and other women?

If you were stronger, what would you do? Could you try doing it anyway?

## power songs

"Empire State of
Mind"
"You Don't Know My
Name"
"Girl on Fire"
"No One"
"Raise a Man"
"If I Ain't Got You"

"Try Sleeping with a
Broken Heart"
"Blended Family
(What You Do for
Love)"
"Girl Can't Be
Herself"
"Diary"

"In Common"
"Karma"
"Teenage Love Affair"
"The Gospel"
"Fallin'"
"How Come You
Don't Call Me"

# ARIANA GRANDE

## Goddess of Evolution

*Ariana Grande* returned to Manchester, England, on June 4, 2017, just thirteen days after a terrorist bombing killed 22 people and injured 116 at her arena show there. This time, the stage was in a different venue—not Manchester Arena but a cricket field two miles away. Still, fifty thousand fans—many of them also attendees at the show that was bombed—gathered to demonstrate that the attack had not scared them into hiding. Ariana, who had just left the arena stage when the bomb went off, showed her solidarity with the audience at the cricket-ground benefit concert, dubbed One Love Manchester, by leading the crowd and herself toward healing.

Though she would continue to suffer from PTSD in the years to come, Ariana anchored a star-filled lineup through the emotional evening. She sang her song "My Everything" with a local school choir. She duetted with

Miley Cyrus on a cover of Crowded House's "Don't Dream It's Over." Wearing a One Love Manchester sweatshirt, she choked up at times while performing her biggest hits as requested by the mother of Olivia Campbell, a fifteen-year-old who died in the attack. Katy Perry, Coldplay, Justin Bieber, Pharrell Williams, Take That, and other acts performed throughout the event. "The kind of love and unity that you're displaying is the kind of medicine that the world really needs right now," Ariana told the crowd.

Ariana Grande-Butera was born on June 26, 1993, in Boca Raton, Florida, to businesswoman Joan Grande and graphic designer Edward Butera. Ariana began performing as a child and got her first break in 2010 as part of the cast of the Nickelodeon show *Victorious*, a sitcom set at a performing arts high school. She played spacey aspiring singer-actress Cat Valentine.

Ariana's solo music career began with the 2011 single "Put Your Hearts Up," a track that she'd later disparage as pandering to the young *Victorious* audience. She made her first effort at an adult music career with her 2013 debut album, *Yours Truly,* which eventually went platinum and included the modest hits "The Way," "Baby I," and "Right There." But 2014 proved to be her breakout year: her sophomore album, *My Everything,* debuted at number 1 on the *Billboard* chart and stormed radio waves with the hit "Problem," featuring rapper Iggy Azalea. Another all-female powerhouse team-up followed on "Bang Bang," which featured Ariana, Jessie J, and Nicki Minaj. Ariana's

2016 album, *Dangerous Woman,* continued her roll, going platinum just like the first two.

Ariana had become an official pop force. Her four-octave soprano vocal range, complete with whistle register, won her comparisons to Mariah Carey. In a 2016 *Time* magazine tribute to Ariana, composer/playwright Jason Robert Brown wrote, addressing her directly: "[N]o matter how much you are underestimated . . . you are going to open your mouth and that unbelievable sound is going to come out. That extraordinary, versatile, limitless instrument that allows you to shut down every objection and every obstacle. That voice—powered by nothing but your remarkable empathy, your ravenous intelligence, your cool discipline and your voracious ambition."

As Ariana's star rose, reports of diva-like behavior began to surface. She didn't get along with her costar on her second Nickelodeon show, *Sam & Cat,* they said. She wouldn't allow a professional photographer to snap her from her right side. Her life coach quit. She demanded to be carried around by her tour manager, they said, when a photo of him doing so surfaced. Her response when asked about some of these rumors in an interview with the *Telegraph*: "If you want to call me a diva, I'll say: 'Um, well, cool.' Barbra Streisand is a diva, that's amazing. Celine Dion is a diva, thank you."

In 2015, security camera footage leaked, showing Ariana in a California doughnut shop licking one of the baked goods and then putting it back, and saying, "I hate America" in response to—she later explained—the large food portions available. She put out a statement afterward: "I am EXTREMELY proud to be an American and I've always made it clear that I love my country. What I said in a private moment with my friend, who was buying the donuts, was taken out of context and I am sorry for not using more discretion with my choice of words." This explained neither the doughnut licking nor the contradiction between her feelings about healthful eating and purchasing doughnuts. But other stars have done worse.

The Manchester bombing changed both her own life and her career. Her first public response came just hours later via tweet: "broken. from the bottom of my heart, i am so so sorry. i don't have words." In the aftermath, she was open about her anxiety but resilient, releasing her musical response to the attack, "No Tears Left to Cry," in April 2018. It appeared on her album *Sweetener*, for which she won critical acclaim and her first Grammy. The album also debuted at number 1 on the *Billboard* chart.

The rest of 2018 continued to be tumultuous for Ariana. She had been dating rapper Mac Miller, with whom she collaborated on her song "The Way," since 2016. They announced their breakup in May 2018. When Miller got a DUI and his fans blamed Ariana online for his difficulties, she responded with a forceful tweet: "how absurd that you minimize female self-respect and self-worth by saying someone should stay in a toxic relationship because he wrote an album about them . . . I am not a babysitter or a mother and no woman should feel that they need to be. I have cared for him and tried to support his sobriety & prayed for his balance for years (and always will of course) but shaming/blaming women for a man's inability to keep his shit together is a very major problem."

Public blame intensified when, by late May, Ariana was dating *Saturday Night Live* star Pete Davidson. They got engaged a few weeks later. That September, Miller died at twenty-six of a drug overdose, causing a new wave of blame to compound Ariana's grief. She and Davidson called off their engagement in October.

Their breakup partially inspired her next major hit, "Thank U, Next," on the 2019 album of the same name. She made the record in just two weeks, ready to pour her feelings into new work. *Rolling Stone* called the result "her best, and most surprising, album to date."

After the agitation of 2018, her songs became more personal in a variety of ways. Her 2019 collaboration with Victoria Monét, "Monopoly," includes Grande singing, "I like women and men." When speculation swirled about it online, a fan tweeted, "Ariana ain't gotta label herself, but she said what she said." Ariana tweeted back, "I haven't before and still don't feel the need to now."

She could say the same about her pop star image overall, which has evolved as she has worked her way through her teens and twenties in the public eye: from child star to diva upstart to a woman who has learned from triumphs and heartbreaks.

## Ariana's Ancient Goddess Sister
# MAEVE

Maeve is the Celtic goddess of cycles and rhythms, and Ariana has experienced her share of those. She has cycled from the highs of chart-toppers to the lows of enduring multitudes of grief in the public eye. She has learned to share her emotions with every step, whether through song or social media, while maintaining her own boundaries. She has talked about her mental health, particularly PTSD after the bombing at her Manchester concert, and has become an unofficial spokeswoman for processing grief. She has made the best of her difficult emotions, pouring them into songs that have given solace to millions of listeners.

## Invoke Ariana for

Enduring trauma

Asking for what you want

Acknowledging anxiety

Standing up for yourself

Refusing to label yourself in any way

## How to channel Ariana's goddess energy

Experiment with a bit of divadom: assert your right to be photographed on your good side, make sure you have your absolute favorite tea, seltzer, and candles on hand. See what feels like the right level of divadom to get your own needs met without hurting others.

Hold a party to celebrate your survival of a difficult event in your life.

Talk to a friend or a therapist about your own anxieties or other difficult feelings.

## JOURNAL RIFFS

How have you evolved over the last ten years?

How have you been underestimated in your life? How did you overcome it?

What was the most pivotal moment in your life so far? How did your actions before, during, and after help you to move forward from it?

## power songs

"Monopoly"

"No Tears Left to Cry"

"Bang Bang"

"NASA"

"Bloodline"

"7 Rings"

"Thank U, Next"

"Break Up with Your Girlfriend, I'm Bored"

"Pete Davidson"

"God Is a Woman"

"Problem"

"Side to Side"

"Dangerous Woman"

# BEYONCÉ

## Goddess of Power Through Sacred Partnership

*Beyoncé appeared* in dramatic silhouette onstage at MTV's Video Music Awards in 2011, then commanded the crowd with a message that had more meaning than the audience initially realized: "Tonight I want you to stand up on your feet. I want you to feel the love that's growing inside of me." In a sparkly purple suit coat, white button-down shirt, and flowy black slacks, she delivered an energetic, 1960s Motown-style performance, backed by lines of coordinated dancers and backup singers, also in suits.

At the end, she dropped the mic, unbuttoned her coat, and revealed her pregnant belly bulging beneath her high-waisted pants.

Beyoncé announced her first pregnancy this way. Beyoncé does everything this way: with drama, flair, style, and an assumption that we're all watching. Because, of course, we *are*.

When Beyoncé went solo with her 2003 album, *Dangerously in Love,* after six years of fronting the successful girl group Destiny's Child, she took a risk. Executives at her record label expressed doubt that there was a hit single among the songs she'd amassed for the effort, to the point where they almost scrapped the album. "Crazy in Love," which was among those songs, would prove this was insane. So would the rest of Beyoncé's career.

Of course, Destiny's Child had enjoyed blockbuster success, and walking away from a sure thing is always terrifying in the entertainment industry. But the success sprang from Beyoncé's undeniable star power and her songwriting. Her growing legions of fans already knew she was a queen. Over time, the world would notice, too, and officially crown her Queen Bey.

It's challenging to write about Beyoncé's goddess powers, because they are so grand and sweeping, which allows them to change depending on the era of her career and the beholder. Her artistry has evolved from the empowering anthems of *Sasha Fierce*-ness (a perfectly valid pursuit) to a much more profound celebration of black, female, Southern American culture that she has used her hit-making power to bring to mainstream white America. (Beyoncé was born in Houston in 1981.) Nowhere was this more evident than when she became the first black woman to headline the Coachella music festival in 2018, turning the set into an hours-long celebration of historically black colleges and universities and including several lines of the song known as the black national anthem, "Lift Every Voice and Sing," with little concern for whether white audiences would get her references.

But like the other goddesses in this book, she has endured major public trials that defined her goddesshood, most notably in her relationship with her superstar rapper husband, Jay-Z. Her astonishing response to years of rumors of his infidelity made her a goddess among goddesses: she remained married to him, then spun the experience into the best work of her career, 2016's visual album *Lemonade*, which used her relationship as a metaphor for the black female experience in America.

She didn't explain herself in interviews, instead allowing the art to speak for itself. When her decision to stay with Jay-Z caused some to question her legitimacy as a feminist leader, she expressed her anger through *Lemonade*'s songs and images (the "Hold Up" clip in which she smashes car windows with a bat comes to mind) and thus reasserted her agency. She came out looking more queenly than ever.

She met Jay-Z when she was eighteen years old, according to her accounts of the relationship. The two began dating when she was nineteen and he was thirty-one. They recorded the duet "'03 Bonnie & Clyde," espousing the ride-or-die mentality that would define their relationship: "When I'm off track, mami is keepin' me focused." The same year, Jay-Z also put in an appearance on "Crazy in Love," with Bey singing, "When you leave, I'm begging you not to go." They made their red-carpet debut as a couple in August 2004 at the MTV Video Music Awards. They married nearly four years later, in April 2008, and revealed they were expecting their first child together at the same awards show in 2011. In January 2012, that

BEYONCÉ

27

child, Blue Ivy, was born. And in June 2014, the couple embarked on their first joint tour, On the Run. Ride or die.

When it came to her father, Beyoncé had a different approach. After he had managed her career throughout her Destiny's Child days and well into her solo life, she split with him on a business level in 2011. The decision proved momentous for her. She made the calls on her next album, and they were unconventional: she dropped *Beyoncé* at the end of 2013 as a complete surprise, and in the process, she changed the industry. Suddenly everyone wanted to do a surprise drop and succeed like her—hardly a sure thing.

By the time she released *Lemonade* in 2016, Beyoncé could do whatever she wanted. She put it out as a coherent visual album on HBO, and the world hung on her every word and image. She told a familiar story about surviving the infidelity of a spouse, lining up with longtime rumors about Jay-Z. More extraordinarily, Beyoncé equated her presumed personal struggle with the larger arc of history for black women in America, particularly in the American South. Just as she struggled to forgive her husband, black women have struggled to forgive America. Beyoncé delivered a vital message at the perfect time.

Meanwhile, she underlined her own commitment to her imperfect husband, staying with him and letting her music speak for itself. He reciprocated with the album *4:44* in 2017, his best in years. If there were a Grammy for inspiration, Beyoncé deserved one for Jay-Z's mature, contrite, introspective work. On *4:44*, he copped to infidelity but also pondered the legacy he would leave his children and opined on the state of black America. He had morphed from the drug dealer–turned-rapper into a grown man, owning his success and its pitfalls, thinking about his place in society, and speaking out. Credit went to Beyoncé for the change.

Beyoncé has shown us the power of collaboration, involving other artists more with every album release. She has made feminism cool. She has demonstrated that women can demand more in terms of pay and professional credit. She has made evident that no artist can please everyone, so you might as well please yourself. She has proven to us that no thigh gap is necessary for success. She has instructed us in the art of creating an alter ego, a Sasha Fierce, to take what is ours. She highlighted the advantages of a masculine side with songs like "Diva" ("Diva is the female version of a hustler") and "If I Were a Boy" ("I'd roll out of bed in the morning / And throw on what I wanted and go"). She articulated the pitfalls of femaleness with songs like "Pretty Hurts" ("Mama said, 'You're a pretty girl, what's in your head, it doesn't matter'").

She offered a seminar on the fine art of stealing a show during halftime of the 2016 Super Bowl, which was headlined by Coldplay. The day before the performance, she dropped the stunning political track "Formation" and its equally stunning video. The song took on extra resonance when Beyoncé and her dancers—all women of color— performed it in the middle of a white, male rock band's

show, the women wearing costumes that evoked the Black Panthers while Beyoncé spit lyrics like, "I like my negro nose with Jackson Five nostrils," and, "I just might be a black Bill Gates in the making."

Despite a subsequent Boycott Beyoncé movement in reaction to the video's messages about police violence against black people and the performance's Black Panther imagery, Beyoncé became the highest-earning female musician in 2017, according to *Forbes*. This was due largely to sales of *Lemonade*, the album containing "Formation," and the Formation World Tour, which took in more than $250 million. Among the tour's merchandise: Boycott Beyoncé T-shirts, which likely made a hefty profit for the star.

As the most goddess-like of the Pop Star Goddesses, Beyoncé appreciates the power of a goddess. She has channeled several in videos and performances, paying tribute to a combination of Indian and Nigerian goddesses during her groundbreaking 2017 Grammy performance, which highlighted her pregnant belly. Similarly, her Instagram photo announcing her second pregnancy echoed images of the Virgin Mary.

Despite her seemingly perfect exterior and her known perfectionist tendencies, she has championed imperfection in her lyrics, from "Bootylicious" to "Pretty Hurts" and "***Flawless." Perhaps that explains the longevity of her sometimes-flawed relationship with Jay-Z. Even her imperfections somehow seem perfect.

## Beyoncé's Ancient Goddess Sister

# MAMI WATA

Beyoncé herself has evoked a number of goddesses in her performances, but Mami Wata is among the most on point for the pop star. An African spirit of water, Mami Wata is usually female in images and stories—but sometimes is male. Several traditions tell stories of her abducting humans while they're swimming, then whisking them off for a spiritual encounter that returns them to their lives looking and feeling better, often even wealthier. She's also linked to both sex *and* faithfulness. Given all this, Beyoncé might just be Mami Wata herself.

## Invoke Beyoncé for

Embracing your queendom

Dedicating yourself to relationships, through ups and downs alike

Breaking free from paternal figures to become your own woman

## How to channel Beyoncé's goddess energy

Be the best at what you do.

Do good in the world.

Celebrate the power of women.

Commit to navigating a relationship's challenges rather than leaving.

Dedicate yourself to your partner.

## JOURNAL RIFFS

How does a current relationship you have—romantic or otherwise—help to fuel your own individual power?

What can you demand that you haven't gotten yet, but know you deserve?

What makes you irreplaceable? What can you do to better project that to the world (or the relevant individuals)?

## power songs

| | | |
|---|---|---|
| "Pretty Hurts" | "No Angel" | "Crazy in Love" |
| "****Flawless" | "Sorry" | "Countdown" |
| "Flaws and All" | "Daddy Lessons" | "Drunk in Love" |
| "Formation" | "Ring the Alarm" | "If I Were a Boy" |
| "Superpower" | "Hold Up" | "Ego" |

# BRITNEY SPEARS

## Goddess of Resilience

*Britney Spears*, a fifteen-year-old who was then unknown to anyone who hadn't watched *The All-New Mickey Mouse Club* in the 1990s, was spending six days a week at a dance studio at New York City's Chelsea Piers to ensure that she'd become an international superstar. Of course, at the time, in 1997, she had no assurances of that happening. She was putting in several hours a day with choreographer Randy Connor—assigned to her by her record label, Jive—to perfect the dance moves and backflips that would conquer the world.

It was time well spent. Two years later, Britney entered pop culture consciousness so fully realized it was as if she had been there the whole time, a seventeen-year-old in pigtail braids and a schoolgirl outfit, dancing with the force of a prizefighter, braying "oh, baby, baby" like a machine. Once you saw the 1999 video for ". . . Baby One More Time," you couldn't remember a time when you

hadn't heard the song or seen those destined-to-be-iconic dance sequences or felt Britney's knowing gaze daring you to love her. But, like most things Britney, the breakthrough resulted from massive amounts of hard work, focus, and determination.

Those four minutes didn't just encapsulate the instant appeal of Britney, who became one of the most successful female pop singers of the twenty-first century when, as *Rolling Stone* said in its online biography of her, she developed "a mixture of innocence and experience that generated lots of cash." The clip also launched the teen pop boom of the 2000s and made MTV's *Total Request Live* a cultural force. That's a lot of power in a short time for a young woman.

The singer, dancer, and sometime actress was born on December 2, 1981, in McComb, Mississippi. She became a child star, going to her first audition for *The All-New Mickey Mouse Club* at eight. The producers didn't choose her then, saying she was too young, but she appeared on *Star Search* to compete as a singer and served as an understudy in an Off-Broadway play along with future star Natalie Portman. (The lead went to Laura Bell Bundy, who eventually headlined Broadway's *Legally Blonde*.) Britney achieved her first level of stardom when she was, at last, asked to join *The All-New Mickey Mouse Club* as a preteen. She ended up being one of several future superstars to populate the show in the early 1990s, along with Christina Aguilera, Ryan Gosling, and Justin Timberlake.

". . . Baby One More Time" and her debut album of the same name made Britney an instant sensation, sparking intense interest in her personal life. She said in interviews that she was a virgin, which set off years of speculation as to whether this was true and, if so, when she would lose her virginity. She had a public romance with fellow former Mouseketeer and heartthrob Justin Timberlake, who had become the breakout member of boy band NSYNC.

But Britney seemed most interested in capitalizing on her moment by releasing new material at breakneck speed. *Oops!. . . I Did It Again* came just one year later, *Britney* the following year, and *In the Zone* two years later, in 2003. Her output gave rise to a barrage of culture-defining moments on par with that first video: the single "Oops! . . . I Did It Again" came with a similarly iconic video, her shiny, red catsuit instantly burned into our brains. *Britney* contained the wildly inventive electro-pop hit "I'm a Slave 4 U," along with another iconic dance video—this time featuring a roomful of sweaty dancers seemingly on the verge of an orgy—only to be topped by Britney performing the song at the MTV Video Music Awards while wrapped in a live yellow python. To support *In the Zone,* Britney returned to the VMA stage, this time to share a kiss with Madonna that made headlines throughout the country. One newspaper, the *Atlanta Journal-Constitution,* even had to apologize to readers after facing backlash for putting a photograph of the kiss on the front page; this only made more headlines.

After *In the Zone*, a tired Britney took a break. Personal drama mounted, as if she'd been putting it off through those years of intense output. After she and Timberlake broke up, media speculation flared. Timberlake fed it by writing a (very good) song about a cheating ex called "Cry Me a River" and cast a Britney look-alike in the video. Britney married a childhood friend on impulse in Vegas, then had the vows annulled. She courted and then married a backup dancer, Kevin Federline, with whom she had two children in quick succession. Now she was even more closely monitored. Thereafter, tabloids pointed out when her complexion was less than clear. Everyone watched and commented as her toned body grew softer.

We were seeing the other face of Britney Spears: not beautiful pop star Britney, but bald breakdown Britney.

This is when her goddess shadow side kicked in.

She had entered the self-obliterating world of show business as a naive teen and a classic people pleaser. "I'm not saying it's good to be a bitch," she said in her 2013 documentary, *I Am Britney Jean*, "but a lot of times in this industry it's better to speak up and say what's on your mind, which I have a problem with." She also said performing allows her an escape from insecurity. But show business itself compounded that insecurity. "She just wanted someone to say, 'I believe in you beyond this pop machine,'" explained songwriter Michelle Bell, who worked with Britney on *In the Zone*, in a 2014 interview with BuzzFeed.

For Britney, her insecurity became a nearly fatal flaw.

She had hinted for years, starting with *In the Zone,* that she was headed for collapse. She cowrote the plaintive song "Everytime," which opens with the plea, "Notice me." Its video depicted her (possibly) committing suicide in a bathtub after being besieged by paparazzi and fans. The video provoked outrage among concerned parents, but no one seemed to worry about what it might be saying about Britney herself.

In December 2004, the superstar personally delivered a just-recorded new track called "Mona Lisa" to a Los Angeles radio station to make sure it would be played on-air. She said it was for an upcoming album called *Original Doll,* and its lyrics told the story of a celebrity who appeared to have died or disappeared somehow: "She's unforgettable, she was a legend though / It's kind of pitiful that she's gone." Her label scrapped the album, and the song was released later with watered-down lyrics scrubbed free of existential angst.

Over the next few years, her public life went haywire. The tabloids critiqued her parenting skills, particularly when she drove with her infant son on her lap without securing him in a car seat. In late 2006 she filed for divorce from Federline. Paparazzi photographed her partying in Vegas with socialite Paris Hilton. Magazines and websites published invasive upskirt photos of Britney getting out of a car without underwear.

Given this context, the 2007 release of her best album to date, *Blackout,* defies belief. But the drama reached an apex around the same time. One day in 2007, she marched into a Los Angeles–area salon and shaved her own head, ridding herself of her signature blond hair in view of clicking paparazzi.

This incident marked the beginning of what *Rolling Stone* called the "most public downfall of any star in history." She followed her public head-shaving by bashing a paparazzo's SUV with an umbrella—this, too, caught on film.

The meltdown made Britney the subject of endless cruel jokes, but it was the ordeal that turned her into a true goddess. Author Tom Payne later compared her public unraveling to the sacrifice of Greek mythology's Iphigenia, whose name means "born to strength." Iphigenia was given to the gods on the eve of war, to which the Greek chorus responded, "And for this, immortal fame, Virgin, shall attend thy name." Payne wrote in his 2010 book *Fame: What the Classics Tell Us About Our Cult of Celebrity* that "her offering has become part of our folk memory. . . . Britney is sacred; 'ordinary people' have made her so."

The meaning of all this comes down, now, to a meme splashed across the internet and etched on coffee mugs for sale via Etsy: "If Britney Spears can get through 2007, you can get through today."

Britney has survived, and this is her miracle. After her public difficulties, legal control of her financial affairs was handed over to her father via a court-ordered conservatorship "due to physical or mental limitations." But Britney,

Inc., has thrived in the years since her breakdown. Her successful line of perfumes has grown to at least twenty-four fragrances, and always counting. Her four-year residency at Planet Hollywood in Las Vegas sold so well, it inspired many of her contemporaries—including fellow Pop Star Goddesses Jennifer Lopez and Gwen Stefani—to seek similar stints on the Strip. Her 2016 album, *Glory,* marked a triumphant return to musical form, combining classic Britney sounds with more modern approaches that sound right at home on streaming services alongside tracks by younger artists like Selena Gomez. True to form, Britney has worked her way back into top dancing shape, embodying the spirit of her 2013 hit "Work Bitch."

Her Instagram feed—which she insisted in a posted video that she manages herself, despite conspiracy theories to the contrary—has become a source of inspiration online. Since late 2016, Britney's hunky trainer/model boyfriend, Sam Asghari, whom she met on the set of her "Slumber Party" video, has appeared regularly. Sometimes with him, and often solo, she posts videos of her impressive workout regime. Her two sons with ex Kevin Federline—Sean Preston and Jayden James—often pop up in or shoot her Instagram photos and videos. "Nothing makes me happier as a mom than watching these boys grow and smile and laugh!!" she wrote in one post.

She's used the social medium to express her admiration for Albert Einstein, post internet-meme inspirational quotes ("Create what sets your heart on fire and it will illuminate the path ahead"), and share video of herself painting pictures of flowers, set to Mozart. (*Lifestyles of the Rich and Famous* host Robin Leach later bought one of her paintings for $10,000, which went to charity.) She often features books she's reading, like *Ugly Shy Girl* (about a teen girl who has a hard time fitting in) and Brené Brown's self-help manual *Daring Greatly: How the Courage to Be Vulnerable Transforms the Way We Live, Love, Parent, and Lead.*

Britney also suffered some public setbacks in late 2018 and into 2019. She had to cancel her second Vegas residency, Domination. She announced that she was taking a break from public life because of the health struggles of her father. She checked into a mental health facility in the spring of 2019. If nothing else, this string of incidents proved the ardor of her fans. Some were so worried about her, they started a #FreeBritney campaign online and even staged demonstrations in West Hollywood, concerned she was being taken advantage of or committed to treatment against her will. Britney stepped in to quell fans' fears, posting Instagram videos to assure them she was cogent and well. Twenty years into her career, her fans still love her fiercely.

So do her peers. Younger artists such as Charli XCX, Julia Michaels, Adele, and the band Haim have professed their fandom, citing Britney as an influence on their careers the way Britney once named Madonna, Janet Jackson, and Whitney Houston as her inspirations.

She lights the way for all of us to survive, thrive, and keep fighting another day, no matter what life throws at us.

## Britney's Ancient Goddess Sister
# ARTEMIS

Among the most popularly worshipped Greek deities, Artemis was a goddess of the hunt, virginity, and childbirth, seen as a protector of young girls. In fact, in some stories, Artemis once saved Iphigenia from being sacrificed by substituting a deer or a goat for the girl on the altar. For these reasons, teenage girls in Athens were sent to Artemis's sanctuary for a year to serve her. In some Greek art, she's even depicted wearing the era's equivalent of a Britney-like schoolgirl kilt, a short skirt that facilitated her hunting. She's often shown holding hunting spears.

## Invoke Britney for

Working toward your goals

Surviving a dark spell

Reinventing yourself

Transforming your health

## How to channel Britney's goddess energy

Work out. A lot. Maybe with your significant other.

Enjoy your Starbucks.

Spritz on some perfume for a boost.

Treat yourself with pizza.

Give up partying and alcohol. Consider a dip in a hot tub or
some yoga to relax naturally instead.

## JOURNAL RIFFS

What do you want? (A hot body, a Maserati?) What must you do to get it?

How are you stronger than yesterday?

Which people in your field can you look to for fresh inspiration?

## power songs

"Circus"

"Work Bitch"

"If I'm Dancing"

"Gimme More"

"Piece of Me"

"My Prerogative"

"Stronger"

"Do Somethin'"

". . . Baby One More
    Time"

"Overprotected"

"Lucky"

"Alien"

"Private Show"

"I'm a Slave 4 U"

# CARDI B

## Goddess of Self-Revelation

*Cardi B had* news to share when she visited *Jimmy Kimmel Live!* in October 2018: giving birth to her first child, Kulture, she said, "broke my vagina." With her hair sleek and bobbed and while wearing a trendy bright blue blazer with matching track pants, Cardi continued: "Why nobody tells you about those things? Nobody told me they were gonna stitch my vagina. People just be like, 'Oh, you know, when you give birth, it's gonna hurt.' But nobody tells you that, like . . . *your vagina.*"

Cardi B became Cardi B just this way. Through sheer force of extreme self-revelation, she pulled herself up from stripper to Instagram star to reality star (on VH1's *Love & Hip Hop*) to one of the most successful rap debuts in history with her 2018 album, *Invasion of Privacy.*

Cardi was born on October 11, 1992, as Belcalis Almánzar, nicknamed Bacardi by her family. Her Trinidadian mom and Dominican dad raised her in the South Bronx, which shaped her Spanish–New York City accent. She grew up in a strict household, but gangs were the currency of her neighborhood. She joined the Bloods when she was sixteen, but she did not find gang life to be as helpful as she had expected. "One thing I could say: Being in a gang don't make you not one dollar," she later said in an interview with *GQ*. "And I know for a fact every gang member, he asking himself, 'Why did I turn this?'"

Cardi started going to college in Manhattan but found it difficult to keep up her studies while also holding down a job as a cashier at the Amish Market. She dropped out, but she lost her job, too. So she worked as a stripper for four years, starting at age nineteen, which she says allowed her to save up enough money to move out of her abusive boyfriend's apartment. While a stripper, she grew a massive following posting on social media platforms Instagram and Vine starting in 2014, which enabled some of her frank posts—mostly about sex and money—to go viral. One of her most popular videos included this monologue: "People be asking me, like, 'What do you does? Are you a comedian or something?' Nah, I ain't none of that. I'm a hoe, I'm a stripper hoe. I'm about this shmoney."

This online popularity led to a spot on the long-running VH1 reality series *Love & Hip Hop: New York*. A *New York Times* article said that on *Love & Hip Hop: New York* "some viewers saw her as a hero of female empowerment, as she made pronouncements like, 'Ever since I started using guys, I feel so much better about myself. I feel so damn powerful.'"

One of her oft-quoted one-liners from the show—"a girl have beef with me, she gonna have beef with me forever"—inspired her song "Foreva," included on her mixtape *Gangsta Bitch Music, Vol. 1.* The website Noisey called *Gangsta Bitch* "easily the most enjoyable body of music to come out of *Love and Hip-Hop*," which, sure, let's take as a compliment. After two seasons, spanning 2015 to 2017, Cardi left the show to focus on her music career. She had at least an inkling that it might work. "I have a passion for music, I love music," she later said. "But I also have a passion for money and paying my bills."

The move paid off: After dropping *Gangsta Bitch, Vol. 2* in January 2017, she was signed to Atlantic Records, and by June, her first single, the profane "Bodak Yellow," went to number 1 on the *Billboard* chart, making her the first female rapper in nineteen years to notch that achievement. Fellow Pop Star Goddesses Nicki Minaj and Missy Elliott, along with other celebrities, celebrated the moment on Twitter. "Bodak Yellow" stayed at the top of the chart for three weeks, giving Cardi the longest run ever for a solo female rapper at number 1.

When her full album, *Invasion of Privacy,* dropped in 2018, it made success look easy, with appearances from high-powered acts such as Migos, Chance the Rapper, and SZA. The follow-up to "Bodak Yellow," "Bartier Cardi," also flew up the charts, dispelling the specter of one-hit-wonderdom. She did it by laying the groundwork for her fame and putting out an album that landed on many critics' best-of-the-year lists. The *Guardian* called it "funny, unapologetically flawed, and instantly quotable." Case in point, the opening track, "Get Up 10": "I started speaking my mind and tripled my views / Real bitch, only thing fake is the boobs."

Cardi B set the mold for celebrity in our time, an actual example of the "authenticity" and "social media platform" marketing wonks dream of. She doesn't just embrace her origin story, in all its messy glory—she built her entire brand on it. In a time when *authenticity* is a buzzword, Cardi doesn't have to try. "I just feel like I influence people because I'm like—I was practically homeless," Cardi said. "A lot of people think dancers don't struggle. We struggle a lot." She has always told her own, honest story through social media. Because followers went along with her from her "regular life" to massive success, she feels even more inspiring. NPR.com named this phenomenon the "Cardi B Effect," describing it as "a branding power rooted in specific authenticity, created and permeated by rapper Cardi B."

Her sister, Hennessy Carolina, is working to become an online influencer in her own right, following in her older sibling's Louboutins. Even after her success, Cardi continued to post videos and photos of herself going without wigs or makeup, bargain shopping, and hanging with family in the Bronx. She remained relatable, even as her own fame now allowed her to meet celebrity royalty. "I'm too nervous, I'm too shy," she told *GQ*. "When I met Beyoncé, people be like, 'How that felt? I bet you was mad happy.' It's like, 'Actually, I wanted to shit on myself.'"

Because of Cardi's transparency, a September 2018 incident in which she threw a shoe at fellow rapper Nicki Minaj at a *Harper's Bazaar* party during New York Fashion Week did nothing to damage her brand—if anything, it enhanced it. This came just a little more than a week after Cardi was involved in a fight with two female bartenders at a Queens strip club, an incident that later resulted in charges of assault and reckless endangerment.

Meanwhile, Cardi's on-off-on relationship with Offset, her husband and the father of her child, has played out on social media like its own season(s) of *Love & Hip Hop.* They got secretly married in September 2017, though, of course, that couldn't stay hidden forever, especially after he "proposed" during one of his shows with an 8-carat pear-shaped diamond ring in October 2017. Cardi soon confirmed that they were already married and announced her pregnancy.

Five months after their daughter Kulture was born, they announced their breakup amid rumors that Offset had been unfaithful. But later that month, December 2018, Cardi shared Instagram photos of tens of thousands of dollars' worth of designer shoes, purses, and jewelry he'd bought to win her back. And they vacationed together in Puerto Rico, which she said via an Instagram video was simply because "I just had to get fucked, that's all. I feel rejuvenated, bitch." Soon, though, sources were telling the tabloids a reconciliation was imminent.

Cardi has also proven to be the perfect star for our time with her fearless embrace of politics and feminism. Her

2019 video with City Girls for the song "Twerk" features shots of women's barely clad asses—including Cardi's—twerking. A lot. Like, for mesmerizing seconds, minutes. It ups the ante on, say, Nicki Minaj's "Anaconda" video and every other empowerment-through-sex clip that's come before it. Conservative critics pounced. "In the era of #MeToo how exactly does this empower women?" writer Stephanie Hamill asked on Twitter. Cardi didn't blink in her reply tweet: "It says to women that I can wear and not wear whatever I want. . . . NO still means NO. So Stephanie chime in . . . I if twerk and be half naked does that mean I deserve to get raped and molested?"

Cardi has voiced her feelings on politics outside her own music videos, too, often speaking out in favor of gun control and against President Donald Trump. "All I'm saying is to admit that your president is fuckin up this country right now!" she tweeted in January 2019. "Liberal or conservative we ALL suffer as citizens." After the school shooting in Parkland, Florida, in February 2018 that killed seventeen people, Trump proposed arming teachers as a solution; Cardi B was not impressed. "When it came to the school shooting, that's when I was like, 'Okay, this nigga really think that everything is a joke,'" she said to *GQ*. "Have you ever shot a gun before? It's very scary and loud. It's traumatizing to shoot somebody. On top of that, what makes you think that a kid wouldn't come behind a teacher, shoot her from the back, then go in her desk and take the gun? And now you got two guns. It's like, 'Don't you calculate?'"

And Cardi's interest extends to political history as well. She's done her homework. Consider that 2018 interview with *GQ* in which she waxed poetic about Franklin Delano Roosevelt as she ate barbecue ribs, brussels sprouts with bacon, mashed potatoes with lobster, and truffle macaroni and cheese with reporter Caity Weaver. "I love political science," Cardi said. "I love government. I'm obsessed with presidents. I'm obsessed to know how the system works." She came with details: FDR got the country through the Depression while in a wheelchair, she explained. "Like, this man was suffering from polio at the time of his presidency, and yet all he was worried about was trying to make America great—make America great again *for real*," she said. "He's the real 'Make America Great Again,' because if it wasn't for him, old people wouldn't even get Social Security."

She further offered that she had learned to list the presidents in order, but said she was too nervous to do it in front of the reporter. She did prove her knowledge of the 22nd Amendment—term limits, y'all—and she offered a surprising depth of trivia knowledge about President Buchanan, our fifteenth. He is known as a historical footnote: the only unmarried president in history.

It has all added up to a new career model as we enter the 2020s: Cardi was worth an estimated $8 million in 2018 and has become a particular source of pride for her community of Bronx Latinas. The *Guardian* called her career trajectory "the new American Dream."

## Cardi's Ancient Goddess Sister
# FREYJA

Norse goddess Freyja embodies bold moves, daring. She encourages us to pursue success by taking risks and all but guarantees we will be victorious. She also tells us to celebrate our hard work with parties and indulgences, something Cardi and her masses of Louboutins represent. In fact, Friday got its name from Freyja—the time to kick back after a week of hard work. When it's time for fun, Freyja says to go all out—flirt, party, enjoy your body, give in to your passion. Or, as Cardi says in "I Do": "Pussy so good, I say my own name during sex."

## Invoke Cardi for

Revealing your true self

Growing a following in your chosen field

Monetizing your strengths and expertise

## How to channel Cardi's goddess energy

Follow your passion, but with a plan to also keep your money flowing.

Embrace social media. Show even the bad stuff. Others will relate.

Get politically active.

Dance, twerk, let it all out.

## JOURNAL RIFFS

What's the scariest thing to reveal about yourself to the rest of the world? What might happen if you did? Can you imagine any good coming out of it, like others relating to your struggle?

What is your calling, your defining mission in life?

What is your relationship to money? Do you welcome it and embrace your need for it, or do you apologize for wanting it?

## power songs

"Drip"

"Bodak Yellow"

"Be Careful"

"Ring"

"Bartier Cardi"

"Money"

"I Like It"

"Motor Sport"

"Foreva"

"Get Up 10"

"Twerk"

"I Do"

# CARLA BRUNI

## Goddess of Rising Above Gossip

*On a* Saturday in February 2008, Carla Bruni put on a knee-length white Hermès dress and exchanged vows with the president of France. The ceremony marked the culmination of a three-month romance, a large portion of which had been captured by paparazzi cameras. This time, no cameras were allowed. The ten-minute ceremony at Élysée Palace made things official between Nicolas Sarkozy, fifty-three at the time, and the forty-year-old model-turned–pop star. The two exchanged rings and a kiss before the mayor of Paris's 8th arrondissement.

With that, Carla Bruni became the first lady of France.

The ceremony wouldn't end gossip about their relationship, which began less than a month after Sarkozy separated from his second wife, Cecilia, who had left him for government relations executive Richard Attias. Sarkozy had taken office in May 2007, less than a year before the wedding to Carla, and every minute had been a tumultuous one for him. He had endured a divorce, his initiatives had stalled, and his flashy style invited criticism—hardly an image a new pop star wife seemed likely to remedy. French papers reported breathlessly about the president's new romance, which included him throwing Carla a fortieth birthday party in December at La Lanterne, the French president's country residence on the grounds of Versailles. Within the first year of his term, several books chronicled the love triangle among Sarkozy, Cecilia, and Carla. Carla, meanwhile, pulled off a personal checkmate, courting the friendship of Sarkozy's first wife, Marie-Dominique, who had been at odds with Cecilia.

Bruni's personal life had long attracted gossipmongers as well, because she had dated rock stars such as Mick Jagger and Eric Clapton. (She was also linked to businessman Donald Trump in 1991, though she later clarified, after he was elected U.S. president in 2016, that she had never dated him. He had spread the rumor himself after his breakup with then-girlfriend Marla Maples.) Carla had her first child, son Aurelien, in 2001 with philosophy professor Raphaël Enthoven, whose father, Jean-Paul, she had dated as well. Oh, and Raphaël was married at the time to Justine Levy, who later wrote a novella that appeared to be autobiographical. The book describes the Carla character, known as "the Terminator," as "beautiful and bionic, with the look of a killer." Around the time when Sarkozy took office, Raphaël told Carla he thought they should separate.

As the *New York Times*'s Guy Trebay put it in 2008, just before Carla's wedding to Sarkozy: "Man trap, serial heart-wrecker, rocker arm candy, photogenic cipher, arrogant heiress, polling gimmick—the woman who appears likely to become the first lady of France has been called a lot of things lately."

Given the keen interest in both of their ongoing romantic narratives, rumors of infidelity plagued the couple throughout Sarkozy's presidency. In fact, the media documented Carla's every move, perhaps even more than an average first lady's. In 2010, for instance, papers reported on her wearing glasses in public for the first time, surmising that she was out to cultivate "a more serious image." Magazines called Giulia, the first child born to a French president in office, in 2011, the "perfect marketing tool" as Sarkozy sought reelection. Commentators speculated Carla would leave Sarkozy once he was out of office. Her response: "Those people who think I love him for his power? Power? They don't understand my psychology at all."

Carla Bruni was born in 1967 in Turin, Italy, to tire company tycoon Alberto Bruni Tedeschi and concert pianist Marisa Borini. The family moved to France when Carla was seven, and she adopted it as her homeland. She dreamed of being a schoolteacher, then a veterinarian, before settling on a music career as her true aspiration. Instead, thanks to her alabaster skin and striking turquoise eyes, she happened into modeling at age nineteen. She catwalked among the top international supermodels during the height of the supermodel craze, from 1987 to 1997.

In 1997, she quit modeling to pursue music. She did so via a deliberate process, starting with going to therapy to overcome what she described as her "narcissism." She parlayed her renown into a career as a singer-songwriter known for her French folk pop and acoustic guitar playing. Her 2002 debut album, *Quelqu'un m'a dit*, hit the top spot on the French charts in its first week and stayed in the top ten for thirty-four weeks.

She recorded her second album, 2007's *No Promises*, in English. Reviewers disagreed on the results. "After the runaway success of her charming, folksy first album *Quelqu'un m'a dit*, Carla Bruni's sophomore effort takes a more difficult route and sees her setting canonical works by such poets as Yeats and Emily Dickinson to music, often calamitously," the website AllMusic said. The *Guardian*'s Liz Hoggard countered, "Poetry set to music can sound hopelessly mannered, but Bruni's songs combine just the right mix of reverence and anarchy." Either way, she had another hit in France and in several other European countries.

In what seems like a surreal move, at least to those of us in America, she released her third album in 2008—

five months after marrying the president of France and moving into Élysée Palace, still in the thick of his presidency. Its title, *Comme si de rien n'était*—which means "as if nothing had happened"—felt, at minimum, ironic. She wrote all the original songs, which included two collaborations with novelist Michel Houellebecq. She canceled an international tour promoting the album because of the enormous security precautions that would be involved now that she was married to the French president. One song's lyrics—in which she describes her lover as "more dangerous than Colombian white"—caused some minor controversy, given her new position. But overall, the record did well in France and earned her another round of admiring reviews. "The Premiere Dame may have a colourful past, but her music has always been as classically chic and subtly sexy as her Christian Dior wardrobe," the *Telegraph*'s Helen Brown said.

Music faded into the background of her life as the first lady, though she occasionally had the chance to merge her dual identities, as when she sang for Nelson Mandela's ninety-first birthday celebration in 2009 at Radio City Music Hall. For the most part, she focused on official duties and charity work, namely protecting mothers and children from HIV.

But as soon as Sarkozy was defeated by Socialist candidate Francois Hollande in 2012, Carla first gave birth to the couple's second child at age forty-four, then put out a new record, *Little French Songs*, in 2013. She said as she

CARLA BRUNI

59

looked back on being first lady in a 2017 *Harper's Bazaar* interview: "It was a fantastic time. Five years of adventure. But I don't miss it." Music became a priority for her upon being freed: "I never stopped writing songs," she said to the *New York Times*. "Music is like a shelter for me—from noise, and from the children. Like a bubble. I have a bubble tendency in any case—that's the way I live. I like loneliness."

In 2017, she returned to full Pop Star Goddess force with her album of jazzy covers, *French Touch*, for which she toured around the world. She slinked her way through the Clash's "Jimmy Jazz," Depeche Mode's "Enjoy the Silence," AC/DC's "Highway to Hell," and the Rolling Stones' "Miss You," among others.

She was, once again, doing what she loved—and, as always, exactly what she wanted.

## Carla's Ancient Goddess Sister

# LALITA TRIPURA SUNDARI

The goddess of erotic spirituality inspires such desire that, according to legend, no one can handle spending even one night in a temple dedicated to her in the Indian city of Varanasi. Priests succumb to their love for her. As the force behind such love, she exerts overpowering creative energy. She also vanquishes demons, just as Carla has defended her politician husband and their relationship in the press. Lalita Tripura Sundari represents the power of sex, love, and pleasure while maintaining a fierce sense of independence. She uses her erotic charms and is skilled at channeling them into fruitful actions. She believes sexuality can be sacred and spiritual, and she easily integrates this with outward grace and charm. She shows up in the architecture of French palaces and Tuscan farmhouses, flowers, and good wine. You can feel her in the heightened energy of a great intellectual discussion.

## Invoke Carla for

Following your heart, whether in love or your career

Bringing grace to positions of power

Dealing with gossip

Bucking convention

Enduring criticism

Shifting careers

Taking risks

## How to channel Carla's goddess energy

Watch Italian films and read Italian books. One of Carla's favorites is the 1954 Roberto Rossellini film *Journey to Italy*.

Watch French films and read French books. Carla liked the recent crime thriller by Fred Vargas, *Quand sort la recluse;* when she goes for the classics, she likes Colette's *La Chatte*, a 1933 novel about the love triangle between a woman, her husband, and his cat.

Indulge in high fashion, even if you can't afford it, by learning about it. Carla is a fan of the Musée Yves Saint Laurent Paris.

## JOURNAL RIFFS

If you were going to record a cover song, what would you choose and why?

If you had one minute left in your life, like in Carla's song "La dernière minute," what would you do with it?

## power songs

| | | |
|---|---|---|
| "Enjoy the Silence" | "Moon River" | "Tout le monde" |
| "Miss You" | "Chez Keith et Anita" | "Le toi du moi" |
| "Crazy" | "Dolce Francia" | "L'excessive" |
| "Highway to Hell" | "Little French Song" | "La dernière minute" |
| "Stand by Your Man" | "Quelqu'un m'a dit" | |

# CARLY RAE JEPSEN

## Goddess of Non-Guilty Pleasure

*Carly Rae Jepsen* has a surefire way to deal with a breakup: wallow a little. She told a fan who asked for advice during the 2017 New Yorker Festival, "I almost try to romanticize it—like, I'm heartbroken and I need a bubble bath and I need wine and I'm gonna listen to really sad music and I'm gonna cry when I need to and I'm gonna talk about it for forever."

Carly Rae made her name singing about the workaday turmoil of young love: in 2011, she rose to fame on the monster single "Call Me Maybe." Yes, the song spread among the masses in part because a bunch of young stars—Justin Bieber, Selena Gomez, and Ashley Tisdale—made a social media video lip synching to it. But it stuck because of that insane catchiness (the BBC called it "more infectious than the common cold") and the relatable sentiment—hoping a love interest will use that number you gave them. It became more than a hit; it was a song you couldn't escape,

a classic Song of the Summer for 2012. She'd gone from a runner-up on *Canadian Idol* to an international star.

She did so thanks to her unique ability to convey the massive drama of the tiniest moments in a budding relationship. "The main inspiration for the song is the idea that there's a kind of chemistry when you meet the right person," Carly Rae told *Seventeen*. "There's a spark that needs to be investigated, but it can be left unsaid because sometimes people are too shy to take that step, including myself. I've never actually asked a guy for his number."

Carly Rae had no idea "Call Me Maybe" would change her life back when she was riffing with cowriter Tavish Crowe in her Vancouver apartment. "It's interesting, the songs that people connect to," she told *Billboard*. "That song, for me, has always been a little bit about how you wish you would have the confidence to act in real life. It's the more fantastical side of things, where you go up to a complete stranger and do something wild that makes you feel alive. I think that everyone has a secret part of themselves that wants to have the confidence to do that."

Such a huge breakout hit often leaves the star nowhere to go but down into one-hit-wonder land. Carly Rae felt it: every subsequent single from that same album, *Kiss*, bombed in comparison.

But she didn't give up. Her 2015 follow-up album, *Emotion*, had critics rapturous, naming it to every possible year's-best list and calling it a "masterpiece." It didn't take off like "Call Me Maybe," but it earned her massive cred. And for her, that was better than ubiquitous fame. She's always avoided the Pop Star Goddess ethos. She has changed her look often, and enough to render her unrecognizable—and not in connection with a new album that required a new vibe, like Christina Aguilera and Taylor Swift are wont to do. "I don't think that I want to feel like because everybody else takes on an identity in the pop world that that's something that I need to do," she told BuzzFeed. "I'm a human being and there's many sides to me, but it's not about creating this larger-than-life image so that it sells better. I find that idea like prison. It sounds exhausting." Her image, she said, was "like a non-pop star; a regular, really boring person."

Instead she relied on her songwriting to make people feel good. She told *Billboard* her standard technique is to look for moments of bliss, write down what they feel like in the moment, and then return to analyze them further once the feeling has worn off. So you're not imagining it: most of her songs deliver shots of euphoria, by design. Writing them gives her a similar high. "I love being on-stage, I love traveling and getting to see the world through music this way," she said, "but nothing beats just kind of being locked up in a studio and writing a song."

Carly Rae Jepsen was born in 1985 in Mission, British Columbia, about an hour's drive east of Vancouver. She sang publicly for the first time at a talent show when she was seven, performing the Bangles' "Eternal Flame." She won four hundred Canadian dollars, which boggled her young mind. At age twenty-one, she was putting together a swing band to perform with when one of her college teachers suggested she audition for the 2007 season of *Canadian Idol*. She felt good about her ultimate third-place finish: "It was like all the exposure without the devilish contract at the end," she said. Her first album, 2008's *Tug of War*, drew on her upbringing with folk-loving parents, influenced by Leonard Cohen, Bruce Springsteen, James Taylor, and Van Morrison. The album didn't make much commercial impact, but the next, 2012's *Kiss*, included "Call Me Maybe"—which, in fact, did start off as a folk song before transforming during the writing process.

After the overwhelming success of "Call Me Maybe," Carly became a favorite of gay audiences thanks to a combination of factors: the video for "Call Me Maybe," which has her hoping an attractive young man will call her, only to see him give his number to another guy in the end; appearances on behalf of causes like marriage equality; and feel-good, danceable tunes perfect for a club. As Michael Waters wrote on Electric Literature, "In queer circles, Jepsen is a cult hero. Numerous queer club nights are thrown in her honor, and sentiments like 'only gays can hear carly rae jepsen songs' and 'carly rae jepsen created gay people when she released "Run Away with Me (2015)"' abound on the internet."

"Run Away with Me" appears among the wall-to-wall irresistible pop tracks on the "Call Me Maybe" follow-up album, *Emotion*. During *Emotion*'s creation, Carly Rae concentrated on making a good album rather than singles. She wrote more than two hundred songs before she chose those that would appear on the record. It worked, as far as critics (and gay audiences) were concerned. She basked in the accolades. She said, "Just because I think of myself probably more as a writer than anything else."

She has allowed ample time between albums to pursue other fun projects. (Yes, they are *all* fun.) After "Call Me Maybe," she did a stint on Broadway as the title character in a *Cinderella* musical, costarring with *The Nanny*'s Fran Drescher. After *Emotion*, she played Frenchy in *Grease: Live* on Fox. She performed the theme song for the 2016 *Full House* reboot, *Fuller House*.

Carly Rae remained grateful for her breakout hit, though she began to regard it as one of the less-fun aspects of her ongoing career. "It's been a game-changer and a life-changer for me and has allowed me the freedom to be able to make albums like *Emotion* without pressure of worrying about anything other than what I want to make, so that's great," she told *Cosmo*. "That being said, I've sung the song a great deal of times, so if you were to ask me to sing any song of my choosing, that probably wouldn't be top of my list just because it's getting a little repetitive to me."

We keep listening not in spite of, but because of, her regularness, her "lovable ordinariness," as *The New Republic* said: "In contrast to modern icons like Lady Gaga, Beyoncé, and Rihanna, Jepsen is just, well, a normie." And that makes her special among Pop Star Goddesses.

## Carly Rae's Ancient Goddess Sister
# OONAGH

Oonagh's motto, according to Doreen Virtue's *Goddess Guidance Oracle Cards*, is "easy does it"—don't fuss, don't force, just go with the flow. Carly Rae has learned to lean into the popularity of her first hit, "Call Me Maybe," without trying to match its success again. Instead, she's focusing on her long-term career and continuing to make quality music that pleases her regardless of chart position. She does what's important to her with conviction, but without straining. She understands consistent progress is better than the extreme highs that have taken other pop stars down. She has faith in her talent. Celtic goddess Oonagh was counted among Ireland's first inhabitants, the Tuatha Dé Danann, who neither ran nor fought back when their land was invaded by the Gaels. They instead turned into leprechauns, which allowed them to remain there peacefully. They became fairies, hiding pots of gold at the end of rainbows and granting wishes—spreading joy, just like Carly Rae.

## Invoke Carly Rae for

Feeling secure in your regularness
Dealing with everyday heartbreak
Embracing all facets of your complex personality

## How to channel Carly Rae's goddess energy

Do something you know will make you feel good, because
it will make you feel good.

Watch a guilty-pleasure movie or TV show.
(*Grease* or *Full House*, perhaps?)

Have a dance party in your living room.

## JOURNAL RIFFS

What are some not-particularly-cool things you enjoy anyway?
Make a list and work your way through doing each of them.

Write with as much drama and emotion as you dare about a
problem you're facing. Be self-indulgent.

Make a list of the contradictory parts of your personality.
Write about one of those contradictions.

## power songs

"I Really Like You"
"Party for One"
"Cut to the Feeling"
"Your Type"
"Boy Problems"
"Curiosity"

"Call Me Maybe"
"This Kiss"
"Good Time"
"Emotion"
"Warm Blood"
"Julien"

"All That"
"No Drug Like Me"
"Store"
"Tonight I'm Getting
   Over You"

## Goddess of Work-Life Integration

*Every night* at bedtime, Celine Dion would gather with her teenage son, René-Charles, and eight-year-old twins, Eddy and Nelson, to say goodnight to a photo of her late husband—their father—René Angélil. As of late 2018, nearly three years after his death from throat cancer, she told *People* magazine she and her sons would talk to René every night and kiss his photo.

Celine has her own private moments with her late husband as well. Before every performance, she holds a bronze replica of his hand and knocks on wood with it for good luck, honoring their decades of success in both love and business—he was her career-long manager. In the studio, she keeps his standard seat behind the sound mixing board open.

No doubt, their romance began with problematic power dynamics. He became her manager when she auditioned for him at twelve years old, though they didn't begin dat-

ing until 1987, when she was nineteen and he was forty-five. They got engaged by 1991. The Canadian star began to break through to American and worldwide stardom the next year when she recorded the theme song to Disney's *Beauty and the Beast* with Peabo Bryson. Celine and René got married in an elaborate Canadian-televised ceremony in Montreal in 1994, marking his third marriage and her first. They gave a press conference before the reception.

In 1998, doctors diagnosed René with the cancer he would battle for nearly two decades with Celine by his side. By this time, their devotion shined brightly: she took two years off from her lucrative career to support him through his cancer treatment, and they renewed their vows in 2000. They welcomed their first son, René-Charles, the next year. The twins were born in 2010.

René's cancer returned in 2013, prompting another career break in 2014 for Celine and a postponement of her Las Vegas residency show. By 2015, she revealed to fans that René was about to die, and that he told her, "I want to die in your arms." They made it to their twenty-first anniversary in December 2015; less than a month later, he died in their Nevada home.

This romance told the entire story of Celine Dion's life: her career and personal lives one and the same, her devotion to them complete. Celine had never known another way of life. She has rarely glimpsed regular, everyday life of the offstage variety. This might be what gives her such a magical, otherworldly quality.

Celine Dion was born March 30, 1968, in Charlemagne, Quebec, the youngest of fourteen children. Her musical family toured Canada as a singing group called Dion's Family, starting when Celine was a baby. The family also opened a piano bar called Le Vieux Baril, where she began performing at just five. She sent a demo tape to Angélil when she was twelve, featuring her singing a song she had written with her mother, and he signed Celine after an audition that made him cry.

She recorded nine French-language albums before she turned eighteen, making her a sensation in her home province. In 1988, she gained worldwide attention when she represented Switzerland—just go with it—in the schmaltzy and beloved Eurovision Song Contest. Her powerhouse vocals won the top prize. She began to learn English and released her first English-language album, *Unison*, in 1990. A few years later, her "Beauty and the Beast" breakthrough helped her 1992 English-language album, *Celine Dion*, sell more than five million copies worldwide. The next year, she kept up the momentum with the release of *The Colour of My Love*, which she dedicated to Angélil.

The 1990s—when she was a well-trained former teen star now in her twenties—became her time to shine. She churned out massive hit after massive hit: "My Heart Will Go On," "Because You Loved Me," "Where Does My Heart Beat Now," "The Power of Love," "That's the Way It Is," "It's All Coming Back to Me Now," "All by Myself."

She became queen of the big soundtrack, with major hits coming from *Titanic*, *Up Close and Personal*, and *Sleepless in Seattle* in addition to *Beauty and the Beast*. By the 2000s, her clout had grown more still: she became a marquee act at Caesars Palace in Las Vegas with a three-year, six-hundred-show, five-night-a-week commitment. The partnership would help to elevate Vegas residencies and would be renewed several times over the next sixteen years. She also signed a deal worth "tens of millions," according to the *New York Times*, to be a Chrysler spokesperson.

Celine had transformed into a commercial juggernaut. She was also—probably not coincidentally—a bit of a joke. She represented the mainest of mainstream, soft-rock, adult-contemporary puffery, according to her critics. To admit to liking her was to admit to uncoolness. Music critic Carl Wilson dedicated an entire 2007 book, *Celine Dion's Let's Talk About Love: A Journey to the End of Taste*, to exploring the tension between fans' passionate love for Celine and critics' hatred of her music.

Wilson comes to a surprising conclusion. Through the course of the book, he develops an appreciation of fans' emotional connection to the singer and even gets choked up himself (at least for a second or two) during one of her Las Vegas shows. "The songs of devotion—'If You Asked Me To' or 'Because You Loved Me'—began to probe at the open sore of my own recent marital separation, and even coaxed a few tears," he writes. "For a few moments, I got it. Of course, then Celine would do something unforgiv-

CELINE DION

75

able, like a duet with an enormous projection of the head of the late Frank Sinatra."

In fact, he argues that critics are the ones with the psychological hang-ups here: "Artistic taste is most competitive among people whose main asset is cultural capital," he writes. "In adult life, it's only in culture-centered fields (the arts, academia) that musical or other culture-centered taste matters the way it does in high school." In other words, Celine's critics need to grow up.

This served not only as vindication for Celine but also as a sign of things to come. In the years since her husband's death, even the cool kids seem to have come around on Celine. The internet has helped, allowing videos of her playful performance and interview personality to circulate. (Nearly every moment she's awake makes for a killer GIF, and she's just as likely to answer a question with an extemporaneous tune as a spoken remark.) Her own social media has allowed humanizing glimpses of her with her sons (celebrating birthdays, enjoying Christmas) and her annual online tributes to her late husband. And let's face it: given the barrage of daily bad news, we could all use a little more cheese.

A headline on a review of a 2017 show in the *Guardian* sums up the shift: "goofy, note-perfect schmaltz goes beyond cool." New Zealand's The Spinoff went a step further in 2018, invoking a modern internet term to review her three-night tour stop at Auckland's Spark Arena: "Celine Dion Is Big Dick Energy."

## Celine's Ancient Goddess Sister
# PARVATI

The Hindu goddess of sacred marriage and devotion, Parvati falls in love with Shiva when she is a young and naive maiden. He has eons of experience, having long ago fallen in love with and/or married Sati—depending on which version of their story you're reading—before she immolated herself. (In some versions, Sati is reborn as Parvati.) At the time of Parvati and Shiva's meeting, Shiva has withdrawn from the world through asceticism, but Parvati brings him back with the power of her love and commitment. Their marriage is fueled by constant exchanges about metaphysics and yogic sutras, an intellectual and spiritual connection. They balance each other. Their union also produces two cosmic-being sons, Ganesha and Kartikeya, and a goddess daughter, Ashokasundari. Parvati represents devotion and fertility. She helps us to find strength, willpower, commitment, and relationship success.

## Invoke Celine for

Integrating your work and home life

Devoting yourself to a relationship

Indulging your schmaltzy side

## How to channel Celine's goddess energy

Go where the money is or play to the crowd. There's nothing wrong with making money or being popular.

Enjoy something you consider a "guilty pleasure," without guilt.

Have a deep conversation with a friend or partner about life, love, or the cosmic universe.

## JOURNAL RIFFS

How can you make your personal and professional lives coexist more peacefully or even work together?

What's one thing you enjoy that's kind of embarrassing to admit? Why is it embarrassing? Could it not be?

## power songs

"Ashes"

"My Heart Will Go On"

"The Power of Love"

"It's All Coming Back to Me Now"

"Because You Loved Me"

"All by Myself"

"A New Day Has Come"

"I Drove All Night"

"Taking Chances"

"Where Does My Heart Beat Now"

"That's the Way It Is"

"Beauty and the Beast"

"Love Can Move Mountains"

"If Walls Could Talk"

"Falling into You"

"Dans un autre monde"

# CHRISTINA AGUILERA

## Goddess of Self-Preservation

*Christina Aguilera* was always so happy to come home from another long day of hot TV lights, screaming audience members, producers' instructions in her earpiece, and dozens of singers vying to inspire her to hit the big button that would make her *Star Trek*–like chair turn around. After hours and hours of this drill as a judge on the TV competition *The Voice*, Christina would get to let go in the soft lighting of her Mediterranean-style mansion, take off her TV makeup and clothes, and blast some hip-hop or Nirvana or Slayer. "Anything like that," she later told *Billboard*, "to get me out of that zone, that TV mode."

She did the *Voice* gig for six seasons, last appearing in 2016, but it makes sense that she was longing to escape it. She started her career on television, as part of the kid cast of *The All-New Mickey Mouse Club* in the 1990s, but even then she was plotting her escape. On her boom box in her family living room, Christina recorded a cover of Whitney Houston's "Run to You," which her manager sent to Disney executives to land her a spot on the soundtrack to

the 1998 animated film *Mulan*. She got the assignment, singing the inspirational theme song, "Reflection." It would become her first of many *Billboard* chart hits, and the first of many escape routes she'd take to get to where she wanted to be—rather than where others wanted her to be—in her career. RCA Records signed her to an album deal soon after.

Christina has yet to repeat the commercial success and cultural command she exhibited in the earliest parts of her career, the "Genie in a Bottle" phase of the turn-of-the-millennium. But she retains respect for her undeniable vocal talent—her four-octave range—and that gives her an endless well to draw upon in pursuit of modest, measured career longevity. "Can Christina Aguilera Reclaim Her (Rightful) Place on the Pop Star Throne?" *Variety* asked in 2018. Writer Jeremy Helligar said the answer was maybe not, because the social media–driven pop landscape favors the new and novel over the tried and true.

But maybe that doesn't matter as long as she can keep finding those escape routes that inspire her—and making music that reflects that inspiration. "When I'm onstage, there's not a bigger high, when I'm in connection with my voice and my heart and my soul," she said.

Christina was born December 18, 1980, on New York City's Staten Island to a musician mother and an army officer father. Her parents divorced when she was young, and she moved around a lot throughout her childhood with her mother. Talented and driven from an early age, Christina became the go-to national anthem singer in Pittsburgh at age eleven, performing before Penguins, Pirates, and Steelers games. She then appeared on the Disney Channel's *The All-New Mickey Mouse Club* for two years, from 1993 to 1995. Throughout, she attended school in Pennsylvania and got her diploma in 1998, finishing her studies with a tutor while she recorded her debut album.

Her career took off right away with the release of that self-titled debut album, as part of the teen pop boom of 1999 ushered in by her fellow former Mouseketeer, Britney Spears. But Christina grabbed every opportunity to put her own stamp on what could have been a cookie-cutter pop career. She didn't play coy about her sexuality the way Britney did; even her first smash single, "Genie in a Bottle," urges the object of her flirtation to "rub me the right way." She recorded a Spanish-language album, *Mi Reflejo,* in honor of her Latin roots. And she took clear control of her music and image with her 2002 release, *Stripped.* She wore chaps and bikini tops, showed off piercings, and smothered her eyes in dark liner. She spoke of abuse she says she and her mother endured at the hands of her father, reflected in songs like "Fighter." She owned her sexual aggression in "Dirrty."

Christina also staked a claim to empowering anthems with "Beautiful" and an accompanying video depicting body dysmorphia, LGBTQ characters, burning magazines full of unrealistic beauty standards, smashing mirrors, and characters of a wide swath of ages and races. In the track "Can't Hold Us Down" with Lil' Kim, she went unapologetically feminist, taking down gender-based double standards and encouraging women to speak up for themselves (the opening verse: "Should I keep quiet just because I'm a woman? / Call me a bitch 'cause I speak what's on my mind"). Both songs came at least fifteen years ahead of their time.

Since then, Christina has cycled through various image changes, married and divorced, had two children, co-starred with Cher in the 2010 guilty-pleasure masterpiece *Burlesque,* and sold more than eighteen million records in the United States alone. She has expertly wended her way among genres and sounds, which her vocal strength allows her to do. She makes a retro, Andrews Sisters–style pop tune funny and dirty with 2007's "Candyman." She wrings tears from her guest appearance on A Great Big World's 2013 breakup ballad "Say Something." She goes pure teen pop on 1999's "What a Girl Wants."

She has arranged her life—with the help of her millions of dollars in earnings, of course—so that many of her needs are taken care of. She didn't have time in her teens to learn to drive, so she's had a driver since her first hits. During one interview piece, a reporter described Christina's assistant preparing the room for the pop star: an iced tea set on a butterfly-shaped coffee table next to a dish of Ricola cough drops and pink crystals, the lights dimmed, a Diptyque candle flickering.

Christina subscribes to a particular kind of feminism

in recent years, one that still incorporates her "Fighter" spirit and her spirit of sisterhood with an appreciation for all things girly. Even at thirty-seven years old, she has still referred to herself as a "girl" in interviews: a "message-T-shirt girl," a "cozy girl," a "girl's girl."

She has spoken out in support of other female stars' attempts to grow as well. In 2019, she praised fellow Pop Star Goddess Lady Gaga in an Instagram post after Gaga apologized for recording a duet in 2013, "Do What U Want," with disgraced R&B singer R. Kelly, who has been charged with several felony counts of sexually abusing underage girls. Christina, who recorded an alternate version of the song with Gaga, tweeted that Gaga was "doing the right thing" by speaking out against Kelly, calling her a fellow "survivor of past predators." Pulling the Kelly version from streaming services while the Christina version remained available, Christina said, served as "a reminder of women sticking together—and not letting a man take ownership of a great song/moment."

Her message has remained the same: "This is who I am, and whoever's not on board can suck my dick," as she said in a 2018 video trailer posted online for fans. But her goddess magic lies in her ability to combine that attitude with a more relatable vulnerability in her messaging and her singing. In the same video, she also admits, "I don't know why we hurt ourselves to please someone else's perception of self. I'm sorry to my own reflection. I'm sorry for putting you down. I'm sorry I struggle accepting the beauty that lies in myself."

The video came as part of her promotion for her 2018 album, *Liberation*, an excellent record that felt unique to her but still at home on current radio, featuring collaborations with several younger stars, including Pop Star Goddess Demi Lovato. Christina found inspiration for *Liberation*, she said, in reigniting the artistic drive of her youth. "To me, the purest of reason is to get back to that little girl who just wants to be inspired again by truth and by that sense of passion for music and singing and just feeling free and alive again," she said in the same video. "I've stepped so far away from that little girl, and if that means going away for a little while and figuring out who you are again and what you need to say, then that's what you need to do."

Christina works best this way, reassessing every few years, and that's why she's always looking for those escape routes. The instrumental title track of *Liberation* features Christina speaking, saying, "Where are you? Are you there? Remember." It feels a little self-indulgent, as many of her albums have—so many songs, so many gimmicky intros and outros. But you can also see why it's necessary for her, especially on the song "Liberation." She is keeping herself focused on what she wants, what she feels, and where she wants her massive career to go next. Her escape routes take her away from the people-pleasing treadmill that trips up many pop stars. If she has to be a little indulgent, a little divaish, to stay on track, then why not?

## Christina's Ancient Goddess Sister
# ATHENA

Athena encourages her followers to listen to their own inner wisdom—"The Voice Within," as one Christina song called it. Athena owns her power and trusts her instincts, and, as a Greek warrior goddess, isn't afraid to fight. The daughter of Zeus, she relies on her brains and talent instead of weapons in battle. Her feud with goddesses Aphrodite and Hera helped start the Trojan War. And while Christina's supposed feuds with fellow goddesses Britney Spears and Pink might be overblown, the online wars among their various fan factions get pretty epic.

## Invoke Christina for

Landing that next-level gig
Following your own path away from what others tell you to do
Building a lasting, satisfying career

## How to channel Christina's goddess energy

Think of something you loved to do when you were little—writing plays, drawing, sculpting with Play-Doh, skipping rope, playing on a jungle gym. Then do it.

Think of something self-indulgent—having a picnic by yourself with a good book, eating your favorite chocolate, taking a candlelit bath, having some tea, reading in bed, taking a nap. Then do it.

## JOURNAL RIFFS

When do you feel your highest high? When you've negotiated a deal at work? When you coached your kid's soccer team to victory? When you're in dance class? Do you have enough of that in your life? Are there ways you can do it more?

What do you want to "escape" to next? How can you get there?

How can you make your primary occupation—whether that's caretaking, art, a career, or something else—your own? How can you put your own unique stamp on what you do?

## power songs

"Ain't No Other Man"
"Dirrty"
"Candyman"
"Save Me from Myself"
"Keeps Gettin' Better"

"Beautiful"
"Can't Hold Us Down""
"Fighter"
"Genie in a Bottle"
"Infatuation"
"Reflection"

"The Voice Within"
"What a Girl Wants"
"Liberation"
"Fall in Line"
"Vanity"
"Accelerate"

# DEMI LOVATO

## Goddess of Fighting Addictions

*Demi Lovato,* at eighteen years old, was already on an international tour with boy band sensations the Jonas Brothers in 2010. She wanted to celebrate during a tour stop in Colombia, so she took her dancers and band out for dinner. She paid for it all—the food, the alcohol. They went back to the hotel afterward and dipped into a stash of weed someone had brought with them. Demi popped some Adderall, her drug of choice at the moment.

By the end of the night, the party group had trashed the hotel room so extensively that the hotel staff alerted the grown-ups in charge of the tour: the Jonas Brothers' dad, Kevin Senior; Demi's stepfather, Eddie De La Garza; and Demi and the Jonases' shared manager, Phil McIntyre. Soon it emerged that one of the dancers had told the men that Demi had been on Adderall. Demi asked Kevin Jonas Senior who it was; she wanted to thank the dancer, she said, because she understood she was trying to help. He bought it and told her: it was a dancer known as Shorty (real name: Alex Welch), whom she'd known for a few years, since they had danced together in the Disney Channel movie *Camp Rock*.

Demi later remembered thinking, "I'm about to beat this bitch up."

Demi boarded the tour plane to the next stop. Shorty had already gotten aboard. Demi walked up to Shorty and punched her in the face. Then she went to her seat, texted her mom "I'm sorry," and fell asleep.

She would end up off the tour and in rehab soon afterward, and again after an overdose seven years later, always in the public eye. Many young, famous performers have gone through a similar ordeal; what is unusual about Demi is how forthcoming she's been about her struggles. "You know, entering rehab while you're on the Disney Channel, it was kind of like, everything was magnified, in the spotlight," she later told *Elle* magazine. "It's quite the headline. And I couldn't get around it. So I thought, you know, I can use this to help others. And that's what I did."

Since then, she's spoken frankly about her addictions to substances, her anorexia and bulimia, and her bipolar diagnosis. She even released a song called "Sober" in 2018, years after the plane incident and a month before her hospitalization for an overdose—and it wasn't a happily-ever-after recovery story. The lyrics: "I'm sorry that I'm here again / I promise I'll get help / It wasn't my intention."

Demetria Lovato was born on August 20, 1992, in Albuquerque, New Mexico, to former Dallas Cowboys cheerleader Dianna Smith and musician Patrick Martin Lovato. Demi loved performing as a child and landed her first role at age seven as part of the cast of *Barney & Friends*, alongside fellow future Disney star Selena Gomez. In 2008, Demi got her major break, costarring with the Jonas Brothers in Disney's hit TV movie *Camp Rock*. She became part of a Disney cohort that would become superstars: Gomez, Miley Cyrus, and the Jonases among them. She even dated Joe Jonas for a few months when they were both teenagers.

But Demi's voice distinguished her from her Disney cohorts and many of the Disney stars who came before her. Her powerhouse vocals put her in the same league as fellow Pop Star Goddesses Christina Aguilera and Kelly Clarkson. Demi translated her *Camp Rock* fame into a recording career, starting with her 2008 debut album, *Don't Forget*, and followed by 2009's *Here We Go Again*. Her musical success even surmounted the Jonas Brothers tour blowup and her rehab stint. A year later, in 2011, she put out another album, *Unbroken*. By 2012, she was judging the TV talent show *The X Factor* alongside Simon Cowell, Britney Spears, and producer L. A. Reid—and Demi was a genuine star, comfortable and witty even on live TV. Keeping up her breakneck work output, she dropped another album, *Demi*, in 2013.

By 2015's *Confident*, she had proven her staying power

and reach as a serious, adult pop star. With that, Demi became the master of owning the worst parts of her life publicly. In a 2016 performance of the powerhouse ballad "Stone Cold" on *Ellen*, Demi seemed to be reliving the heartbreak behind the lyrics, which describe the struggle to be happy for an ex who's moving on. In 2017, she executive-produced a documentary called *Beyond Silence*, depicting the lives of people with mental illness, including schizophrenia, bipolar disorder, depression, and anxiety. At the 2017 American Music Awards, her performance of her song "Sorry Not Sorry"—an otherwise upbeat post-breakup anthem from her album *Tell Me You Love Me*—included projections of scathing real social media messages that had been directed at her: "Fat rat, u deserve nothing," "you're ugly," "piece of trash." In 2018, she choked up onstage while singing a spare version of "Sober," accompanying herself on piano.

Demi has weathered at least a pop star's share of online abuse, if not more. Some internet users seem to enjoy making lists of reasons to hate her. She committed a minor gaffe in 2019 by saying she enjoyed some of the (not particularly mean-spirited) memes that spread online after the arrest of British rapper 21 Savage on immigration charges. (She posted one poking fun at his Britishness, showing the arm of a man in Victorian-era dress writing with a quill, with the caption "This is how 21 Savage be writing his verses.") At a time that was just seven months after her hospitalization for an overdose, commenters responded, "Go shoot some more heroin," "She's a crackhead," and "Rehab doctors better take her phone away."

Demi has had an on-and-off, love-hate relationship with social media, often announcing extended breaks when things get too intense. But when on social media, she commits 100 percent. She doesn't mind tweeting about her anti–Donald Trump political beliefs or posting a shot of herself in a bikini while pinching a bit of her own flesh. But she has used it most effectively when communicating with fans about her struggles. Just weeks after her 2018 overdose, she posted on Instagram: "I have always been transparent about my journey with addiction. What I've learned is that this illness is not something that disappears or fades with time."

She explained her social media strategy to Canada's *Breakfast Television*: "At the end of the day you have to realize that people can't relate to glamour all the time. You can give people an insight into how rad your life can be, sometimes, as a pop star, but also to share who you are with them is important so that they can relate as well."

In fact, she has even revealed the times when glamorous events weren't nearly as fun as they looked from the outside. She attended the high-fashion Met Gala in 2016 for "my first and probably last" time, as she posted afterward on Instagram, accompanying a photo of herself looking awkward on the red carpet while Nicki Minaj appears to roll her eyes at Demi from nearby. "It was very cliquey," Demi told *Billboard*. "I remember being so uncomfortable that I wanted to drink."

Instead, she said, she left to find an Alcoholics Anonymous meeting. "I changed my clothes, but I still had my diamonds on—millions of dollars of diamonds on in an AA meeting," she said. "And I related more to the homeless people in that meeting who struggled with the same struggles that I deal with than the people at the Met Gala—fake and sucking the fashion industry's dick."

This attitude comes from a core philosophy Demi has developed for a life in the spotlight: "I'd rather live my life free and open than closed off, where people like me for something that I'm not," she told Refinery29. She doesn't reserve her radical candor for others, either; she's just as happy to tell on herself. "Prior to getting sober, I was one of those people who was like, I don't give a fuck, whatever," she said in 2016. "And I used that as an excuse to do whatever I wanted. I was a nightmare to work with."

She has since forgiven herself, though. In 2019 she posted a photo to Instagram of a bouquet. "'Cause sometimes you gotta send yourself flowers," she captioned it. This self-regard has kept her alive and well—and successful—for this long. Her struggles may continue, but her strength always wins in the end.

## Demi's Ancient Goddess Sister
# GREEN TARA

Green Tara encourages us to ask for help, which is what Demi has continued to do to fight her own addictions. Demi has, at times, given in to her compulsions, looking to soothe herself when she feels overwhelmed. But she has also learned, over the years, that she cannot fight her demons alone. Green Tara represents a strong mind and an open heart, which is what Demi has maintained in the moments she has saved herself by reaching out. Hindu and Buddhist goddess Tara comes in several different colors, with green representing emergency help and empathy. She helps her followers to save themselves.

## Invoke Demi for

Fighting your own recurring demons
Asking for help
Sharing your struggles with others
Handling the negative side of social media
Owning up to your faults

## How to channel Demi's goddess energy

Send yourself flowers with a love note.
Apologize to anyone you've wronged.

## JOURNAL RIFFS

What do you need "rehab" for? It doesn't need to be a major addiction, though if it is, seek help. If it isn't, how can you come up with your own program to quit eating too many sweets, binge-watching too much TV, or whatever your destructive vice is?

What is a less-than-perfect life moment or struggle that you could share on social media for the benefit of others?

## power songs

"Daddy Issues"
"Sorry Not Sorry"
"Sober"
"Stone Cold"
"Tell Me You
   Love Me"
"Confident"

"Cool for the
   Summer"
"Heart Attack"
"Neon Lights"
"Skyscraper"
"Give Your Heart a
   Break"

"This Is Me"
"You Don't Do It for
   Me Anymore"
"Body Say"
"Remember
   December"
"Lonely"

# GWEN STEFANI

## Goddess of Following Your Muse

*Later it* would seem ironic that Gwen Stefani was onstage at the Grammys in 2015, in front of an orchestra and opposite Maroon 5 lead singer Adam Levine, singing a ballad about the vulnerability of love, "My Heart Is Open." But at the time, it was business as usual, two pop music veterans doing their thing, Gwen in her go-to Old Hollywood glamour look: platinum hair coiffed and pulled back, red lipstick matching her red, strapless gown with a slit that reached her upper left thigh.

Less than twenty-four hours later, her life, carefully constructed over the previous decade-plus, lay in wreckage. She and her husband of thirteen years, rock star Gavin Rossdale, had hit what turned out to be an impasse in their relationship. The morning after the Grammys, as Gwen has (sort-of) told the story in interviews, she found out something that would cause the relationship irrepa-

rable harm. She declined to elaborate publicly on what caused the split, saying she wanted to protect their three sons. The tabloids, however, agreed that Rossdale had been cheating on Gwen for years with the family's nanny.

This moment counted among a handful of inflection points in a career built on Gwen's unique combination of what some would call contrasting qualities. She represents the ultimate girly girl who has spent her career hanging with the boys in her band; she's sometimes a rock star with a pop accessibility, other times a pop star with a rock edge. She wrote and sang the feminist pop anthem (or as close as we could get to one on mainstream radio in 1995) "Just a Girl" and has rarely been without a steady, high-profile man throughout her adult life in the spotlight. She symbolizes female empowerment, though she has never hidden her adherence to some of the conservative values of Orange County, California, where she grew up—her lyrics long for a settled-down, American Dream life with a husband and kids. And she has often spoken about keeping a low profile, staying out of the tabloids and maintaining a private life, while always, in the end, drawing on that private life for her songs.

All these contradictions made her 2015 Grammy moment, and its tabloidy aftermath, and the songs that would eventually come out of it, a particularly compelling chain of events.

Gwen Renee Stefani was born on October 3, 1969, in Orange County and raised there as part of a Roman Catholic family. In 1986, when she was seventeen, her brother Eric formed a ska band, No Doubt, and asked her to be the lead singer. Soon after she joined, she began dating bassist Tony Kanal.

Gwen became the mainstream version of a specific kind of 1990s girl. While Riot Grrrl bands celebrated, in great detail, their right to swear, fuck, scream through their songs, and fight against gender norms, Gwen sang, "I'm just a girl, all pretty and petite / So don't let me have any rights / Oh, I've had it up to here!"

While the Riot Grrrl bands and their fans made zines and designed their own clothes, Gwen ripped up and bejeweled tank tops, cut up thrift store finds to suit her needs, sewed some of her own clothes, dyed her own hair, did her own stage makeup, and used stick-on earrings as a bindi in homage to Kanal's Indian mother. The difference: No Doubt was on tour opening for the international sensation Bush and making videos for their major-label debut album. "I mean, I'm very vain," she later said. "That would be my middle name. Of course I am, you know what I mean? I love the visual."

In 1995, when she and her band, No Doubt, played a *Roe v. Wade* benefit concert for Rock for Choice, she shocked the organizers by saying from the stage, "If I got pregnant right now, I wouldn't get an abortion. But isn't it cool that nobody can tell me what I can and can't do?" It seemed she was not supposed to be a rock star who wanted babies, who wouldn't

choose abortion for herself, but also wanted other women to

have that choice. The public, of course, didn't mind one bit; over the next few years, *Tragic Kingdom*, No Doubt's third album, would go ten-times platinum.

Her political fence-straddling hasn't aged perfectly. As America's political climate grows more dire, Gwen has remained apolitical, and her penchant for adopting the visual markers of other cultures—wearing an Indian bindi, or sporting a Native American headdress, or adopting a troop of Harajuku girls as an entourage—has come to be recognized as careless appropriation. In the 1990s one could see the advantage of making feminism a little more palatable, showing even the sweetest, least angry girl-next-door could be a feminist. Now these choices look like a willful decision to ignore the world from a position of privilege.

Still, No Doubt in the 1990s and 2000s built itself on Gwen's image, carefully (and profitably) walking the line between respected rock and accessible pop. Their video aesthetic centered on Gwen; their lyrics were her most personal thoughts, fueled by an angsty breakup with Kanal. By 2001, the band reached a chart-dominating zenith with the album *Rock Steady*.

At that point, No Doubt went on a hiatus as its members tried their hands at constructing adult lives. And by 2002, Gwen had built the life she wanted, the American Dream with a few rock star rips in its designer jeans. She married her boyfriend of seven years, Rossdale, the lead singer of Bush. They had three kids. She started a high-end fashion line, L.A.M.B., and its lower-priced counterpart, Harajuku Mini, which gave her another way to show her, let's say, *interest* in the aesthetics of other cultures; her rarefied life seemed to make her ignorant of, or indifferent to, criticism that she was commodifying, say, Japanese Harajuku girls in a thoughtless way.

In 2004, she added another puzzle piece to her carefully constructed image: she released her first solo album, *Love. Angel. Music. Baby.* It spawned hits as easily as No Doubt's records had, including the instant nonsense-pop classic "Hollaback Girl." Gwen said she knew as soon as she wrote it with producers Chad Hugo and Pharrell Williams that it was a winner: "We were jumping all over the couch, we were doing the Tom Cruise, we were like, '*Ahhhhh!*'"

Two years later, she released another album: *The Sweet Escape.* After she toured to promote *The Sweet Escape*, No Doubt put out their first album in more than ten years, *Push and Shove*, in 2012. Gwen made it clear she had no intention of quitting the business until it kicked her out: "Music has this emotional thing to it, and it touches people in crazy ways," she said. "The power of *having* that power is something that, once you have it, you don't want it to ever end."

She sought to share that power with up-and-coming artists as she joined *The Voice* in 2014 as a celebrity coach, alongside her sometime collaborator Pharrell Williams as well as stalwart coaches Levine and country star Blake Shelton.

After she and Rossdale split in 2015, Gwen added yet

another contrast to her collection: she began dating Shelton during *The Voice*'s ninth season. At first, coverage of the couple focused on their sitcom-style differences: he's a little bit country, she's a little bit rock 'n' roll! But in some ways the coupling made more sense than many of her other choices throughout her public life. The two shared traditional values, including a churchgoing habit. And when she absorbed some of his country roots into her revolving lineup of looks, for once, her adoption of a new subculture didn't read offensively. The cowgirl outfit she added to her Las Vegas residency show was one that presented zero problems for a white American woman.

The breakup with Rossdale and new love with Shelton also returned Gwen to her confessional songwriting with her third solo album—her first in ten years. But it marked a turn for her solo career, which had so far churned out more fun dance tunes than personal expressions. She described a call with executives at her record label as feeling like "five people punching me in the stomach." During it, she said she was told, "We support you, you should put out an artistic record, and don't go for radio. It's over for you, basically." This did not sit well with Gwen, who was not interested in this so-called artistic record idea: "Once you have a hit, there's not much point in ever writing a song that doesn't have the intention of being a hit," she said.

John Janick, the chairman and chief executive of Interscope Geffen A&M, later recalled that conversation: "I said, 'I'm not sure you have the song that's going to

really connect with people.' And two days later, she sent us 'Used to Love You.'" That single peaked at number 20 on the *Billboard* chart—not the kind of dominance Gwen once enjoyed, but respectable. However, the album itself debuted at number 1 on the *Billboard* chart. She was still officially a hits girl.

*People* magazine called 2016's *This Is What the Truth Feels Like* "a personal and artistic triumph" that allowed her to publicly work through her recent turmoil. She sings on the song "Truth": "And they're all gonna say I'm rebounding, so rebound all over me / 'Cause I don't want nobody else." Gwen didn't play coy about the album's subject matter: "I would consider it a breakup record," she said. "It just makes me believe in God and my journey. My cross to bear was to go through these heartbreaks and write these songs and help people." *Entertainment Weekly*'s Leah Greenblatt echoed the accolades, saying the album included "some of her most purely satisfying pop songs in years."

The reviews didn't come in universally positive, but Gwen said all she could do was follow her inspiration and recognize the realities of aging as a pop star. "It's a natural thing to think about, your evolution," she told the *New York Times*. "I had a lyric, 'Born to blossom, bloom to perish,' and how in nature you see it all the time. We're just born to die. You can think of it like it's a tragedy or you can think about it like, you're gaining something all the time and you're losing something all the time, but you're finding out what is the truth, what is important."

# Gwen's Ancient Goddess Sister
## SITA

Sita is, according to Sally Kempton's *Awakening Shakti,* the Hindu "goddess of devotion and mystical submission." Gwen has always followed her heart in love and work, and has often found the two intertwined: as her personal life surges, so does her songwriting drive. Sita endured her own, ancient-goddess-level domestic and romantic drama: when her husband, Rama, was banished to the forest by his stepmother, Sita insisted on following him into exile. In the forest, the two were taunted by a demoness who had fallen in love with Rama and by the demoness's evil demon-king brother, Ravana. Ravana kidnapped Sita to be his own, but Sita refused to give in to his advances, declaring fidelity to her husband, Rama. Even while imprisoned and threatened with death, she remained loyal. But when Rama found her and rescued her, he refused to reconcile with her. He believed she must have given in to Ravana and was therefore "impure." She proved her purity by building a fire and praying to the god of fire, Agni: "Since my heart has always been true to Rama, give me your protection." She stepped into the fire, remained for a bit, and then stepped out again, unscathed. Rama believed her, and they reconciled. Sita embodies traditional feminine devotion; she is the woman who is so entwined with the men in her life that they are her weak-

## Invoke Gwen for

Recovering from a broken relationship
Embracing your contradictory qualities
Integrating your masculine and feminine sides

## How to channel Gwen's goddess energy

Go thrift store shopping to change up your look.
Draw, paint, or express yourself artistically in whatever way you please.
Experiment with makeup.

## JOURNAL RIFFS

Who or what is your muse? Even if you don't write or make art,
who or what inspires you to come up with new ideas or do your best?
Write about it.

Imagine the ideal version of the person you want to be. How could you
express that identity through fashion, hair, or makeup?

What's the biggest seeming contradiction in your personality and values?
How do you make sense of that contradiction?

## power songs

"What You Waiting For?"
"Orange County Girl"
"Yummy"
"Don't Get It Twisted"
"Used to Love You"

"Simple Kind of Life"
"Hella Good"
"Hey Baby"
"Underneath It All"
"In My Head"
"Just a Girl"
"Bathwater"

"Running"
"Spiderwebs"
"Don't Speak"
"Ex-Girlfriend"
"Make Me Like You"
"Truth"

# JANELLE MONÁE

## Goddess of Coming Into Your Own

*Janelle Monáe* lies on what looks like a floating exam table, dressed in a white and gold bikini, a white plastic helmet resting atop her braided hair. A disembodied voice commands her to repeat: "I am a dirty computer. . . . I am ready to be cleaned." Janelle repeats, "I am a dirty computer," but she cannot—will not—say that she is ready to be cleaned, that is, to have her thoughts, feelings, and memories erased so that she is just like everyone else.

This scene opens the "emotion picture"—the movie-length video, a form Janelle pioneered on previous albums, even before Beyoncé did so—that accompanies Janelle's 2018 album, *Dirty Computer*. It means to be a culmination of Janelle's four-album career thus far, the moment when her alter ego, an android she calls Cindi Mayweather, becomes a real woman, the artist Janelle Monáe. But even if you haven't been following the complicated Afrofuturist backstory she has constructed, you get the idea: Janelle

is owning all the faults, quirks, and qualities that make her different from the mainstream. She is integrating her true self with her art.

"I got to the point where it was crippling me, this idea of perfectionism, and it stopped me from writing for a minute," she told NPR. "And what I decided to do was take some time. So when I wrote this album, it wasn't about perfection. It was about the imperfections. It was about embracing all those things that make you unique, even if it makes your own self uncomfortable."

This inflection point came amid a journey she had begun with her 2007 EP, *Metropolis: Suite I (The Chase)* and her 2010 debut studio album, *The ArchAndroid*. The music and its accompanying videos tell a story inspired by the 1927 German sci-fi film *Metropolis*; in Janelle's narrative, Cindi time travels from the future to the past to free the citizens of Metropolis from a surveillance state that suppresses freedom and love. Her musical influences added to the sense of high-concept eclecticism, mixing, as she said, elements of traditional film scores with hints of David Bowie, Stevie Wonder, and OutKast.

Pitchfork's Matthew Perpetua called *The ArchAndroid*, which included the Barack Obama–inspired hit "Tightrope," "about as bold as mainstream music gets." He wrote, "Her imagination and iconography deepen the record as an experience and give her license to go far out, but it ultimately serves as a fun, flashy framework for pop songs with universal lyrical sentiments. . . . As with all the musi-

109

cal genres blended into *The ArchAndroid*, Monáe uses the conventions of science fiction as a means of communication, tapping into mythic archetypes for their immediate resonance and power." *URB* magazine called it a "genre-defying masterpiece."

*The Electric Lady* in 2013 continued the *Metropolis* story and hinted at what was to come. The single "Q.U.E.E.N.," initially titled "Q.U.E.E.R.," included the telling lyric, "They call us dirty 'cause we break all your rules down." But it took until 2018, with *Dirty Computer*, for Janelle to find herself in Metropolis. "I knew I needed to make this album," she said, "and I put it off and put it off because the subject is Janelle Monáe."

Janelle Monáe Robinson was born on December 1, 1985, in Kansas City, Kansas, into a sprawling Baptist family that believed, among other things, that all gay people go to hell. "I got 50 first cousins," she later explained to *Rolling Stone*. She grew up in the area's working-class neighborhood of Quindaro. As an escape from the realities of her family, she would dream of other worlds.

She performed throughout her childhood and, after graduating from high school, enrolled in the American Musical and Dramatic Academy in New York City. However, she found the curriculum's focus on performing classic plays limiting; she wanted to write her own material. So she dropped out and moved to Atlanta, where she lived in a boardinghouse with six other women and got a job at Office Depot.

Janelle got her first break when OutKast's Big Boi caught her performance of Roberta Flack's "Killing Me Softly" at an Atlanta open mic in 2005. He asked her to sing on a handful of the rap duo's songs, including "Call the Law" and "In Your Dreams" on their 2006 album, *Idlewild*. Then she began work on *Metropolis*, developing both the Cindi alter ego and a signature look: she always dressed in black-and-white, tuxedo-inspired outfits to pay homage to her working-class parents, a custodial worker and a garbage man, who both wore uniforms. This also served as a statement on the fluidity of gender: "I feel like I have a responsibility to my community and other young girls to help redefine what it looks like to be a woman," she said. "I don't believe in men's wear or women's wear. I just like what I like," she told Gizmodo in 2010.

The cumulative success of her four albums, plus high-profile roles in the 2016 films *Hidden Figures* and *Moonlight*, made Janelle a major pop cultural force by 2018. She told *Fast Company* she had to take a hard line on collaborations with others: "One of my biggest strengths is I'm unafraid to say no. I'm not into people owning me. I have a strong vision, and any companies or partners who want to work with me have to match my purpose: shaping culture, redefining culture, and moving culture forward."

As she promoted her first personal album, *Dirty Computer,* she dropped her black-and-white uniform, came out as pansexual, and delivered a forceful introduction to

fellow Pop Star Goddess Kesha's emotional performance of her survivor-empowerment anthem "Praying" at the 2018 Grammys: "We come in peace," Janelle said, "but we mean business. And to those who would dare try to silence us, we offer two words: time's up."

In the *Dirty Computer* era, she became a feminist and queer idol. The album and its accompanying video celebrate women—and specifically vaginas—repeatedly. The song "Pynk," an ode to female genitalia, makes this manifest with a video clip featuring Janelle and her dancers in puffy pink pants that evoke labia. The full-length film includes a love story between Janelle and a character played by actress Tessa Thompson, sparking online speculation that the two were a couple. During an interview with *Rolling Stone*, Janelle came out for the first time, with this iconic quote: "Being a queer black woman in America, someone who has been in relationships with both men and women—I consider myself to be a free-ass motherfucker."

BuzzFeed declared 2018 "the year of the queer woman pop star," citing Janelle as a prime example. The UK's *Independent* described *Dirty Computer* as the "perfect celebration of queerness, female power, and self-worth." None of this stopped the album from receiving mainstream acclaim, including an Album of the Year Grammy nomination and mentions on more than a dozen major best-of-the-year lists.

*Rolling Stone* called the full-length video a "sci-fi masterpiece" and a "shrewd commentary on present-day America." The *Guardian*'s Kitty Empire echoed this sentiment when reviewing the music, explaining how one song in particular reflected the era: "The track 'Django Jane,' released a couple of months ago, best displays Monáe's fearlessness: every rapped line is barbed and brilliant, taking in her background, her success, its possible tokenism ('Prolly give a Tony to the homies') and concluding with a salvo on behalf of creative black womanhood; even calling it 'a salvo on behalf of creative black womanhood' can't kill how great her flow is here."

She has transformed from an android into a Pop Star Goddess who celebrates womanhood, blackness, queerness—and a future in which we all feel like we belong, not in spite of our differences, but because of them.

## Janelle's Ancient Goddess Sister
# AERACURA

Aeracura represents blossoming, according to Doreen Virtue's *Goddess Guidance Oracle Cards*, and that is what Janelle Monáe did before our eyes over the course of her first four albums. It took her a while to own her full, true identity, and as a result we got to see the process unfold—which makes her the perfect goddess for any of us as we continue to evolve. The journey proves the point. Along the way, you learn new things, find new inspirations, and grow until it's time to unleash your full power onto the world. She shows us that you can be patient with yourself and take life as it comes, nurturing yourself and maintaining faith in yourself along the way. Aeracura herself is a Celtic and German goddess who is a fairy queen and a bridge between the earthly realm and heaven, just as Janelle is an emissary of an alternate Afrofuturist realm but grounded in the realities of our world.

## *Invoke Janelle for*

Resisting conformity
Innovating
Becoming your authentic self

## *How to channel Janelle's goddess energy*

Take up a hobby you're not that good at, and probably will never be that good at, just to practice being imperfect.

Take a class in something you know nothing about, just to learn.

Create an alter ego. Give her a name and imagine her as fully formed as possible. Spend a day acting like her.

## JOURNAL RIFFS

Whom do you see yourself becoming in ten years? Write out a full description of this life: Where do you live? With whom do you spend most of your time? What do you wear? What do you do for a living?

Create your own alternate sci-fi universe. Who is in charge? What are the beings like? What do they wear? What do they do for fun? What are their biggest challenges? Go as far as you can.

What does being a free-ass motherfucker mean to you in your own life?

## power songs

"Tightrope"
"Crazy, Classic, Life"
"Take a Byte"
"Screwed"
"Django Jane"

"Pynk"
"Make Me Feel"
"I Got the Juice"
"Don't Judge Me"
"Americans"

"Q.U.E.E.N."
"Electric Lady"
"PrimeTime"
"Dance Apocalyptic"

# JENNIFER HUDSON

## Goddess of Grace Through Highs and Lows

*A tearful* Jennifer Hudson accepted her 2007 Oscar from presenter George Clooney, then choked out, "I have to just take this moment in. I cannot believe this." She added, "Look what God can do." She was competing against the likes of Cate Blanchett and had won for her first professional acting role, so Jennifer's victory for *Dreamgirls* was no small accomplishment.

Her journey to this moment had proven even more remarkable. She had placed seventh on the 2004 season of *American Idol*—and, let's face it, history does not normally remember the seventh-placers. In *Dreamgirls,* she once again played the runner-up, this time as Effie White, a singer in the fictional girl group the Dreamettes who is sidelined to spotlight the slimmer Deena, played by superstar and fellow Pop Star Goddess Beyoncé. Jennifer beat out nearly eight hundred other hopefuls to get the role.

If awards were going to be her motivator, she was already finished. She had peaked. To continue with her career, she'd have to find a more internal source of motivation. "Even though I am extremely blessed to have accomplished many of my goals at such a young age, I am still reaching, still striving," she said.

Jennifer Kate Hudson was born on September 12, 1981, in Chicago. Raised as a Baptist in the city's Englewood neighborhood, she grew up singing in the church choir and performing in local theater productions. She would sit on the steps of her home and sing into a hairbrush, idolizing Aretha Franklin. Jennifer later said, "I owe my mother everything. I wouldn't be where I am today if she hadn't been there to raise me right."

Jennifer rose to national prominence as a finalist on the third season of *American Idol*, a megahit that had taken over television in 2004. She auditioned in Atlanta, telling the judges she had been singing on Disney Cruise Lines as one of the Muses from *Hercules*. Judge Randy Jackson said, "We're expecting more than a cruise ship performance from you." They got it: she delivered a flawless rendition of Aretha Franklin's "Share Your Love with Me" that changed Jackson's skeptical tune. "Brilliant," he said. "Absolutely brilliant. The best singer I've heard so far." However, Jennifer became emblematic of the show's major flaws: judge Simon Cowell's bullying tendencies disguised as honesty ("At the time, Simon told me I was 'too big, in every way,'" Jennifer later recalled), and the limits of the audience-voting format (that seventh-place finish, despite her being a clear standout as a vocalist).

Jennifer's career immediately following proved *Idol* results do not always correlate with real-life success. Her eponymous first album in 2008 debuted at number 2 on the *Billboard* chart, earned several Grammy nominations, and won the award for Best R&B Album. She sang the national anthem at the Democratic National Convention in August 2008 at candidate Barack Obama's request. And then there was the Oscar thing.

But unthinkable tragedy interrupted Jennifer's post-*Idol* fairy-tale career: in 2008, just as her debut album was taking off and she was appearing in the first *Sex and the City* film, her mother, brother, and seven-year-old nephew were shot and killed by her former brother-in-law in Chicago. (William Balfour was convicted of the crime in 2012 and sentenced to life in prison.) "Nothing is just," she would later say. "Everything leads to something else."

For her, that "something else" included an engagement to pro wrestler and actor David Otunga and the birth of their child, David Jr., in 2009. Over the next two years, she lost eighty pounds, which landed her an endorsement deal with Weight Watchers. She wrote a bestselling memoir, *I Got This: How I Changed My Ways and Lost What Weighed Me Down.* Movie roles continued to come her way as well, including *The Secret Life of Bees, Winnie Mandela, The Three Stooges, Black Nativity, Chi-Raq,* and *Sandy Wexler.* She also appeared on television in recurring roles on *Empire* and *Smash,* and on Broadway in a musical adaptation of *The Color Purple.*

The tragedy fueled her political stances. She performed "The Times They Are a-Changin'" at the 2018 March for Our Lives, supporting gun control. She referenced her own experiences when she spoke at the rally: "To me," she said, "the saddest thing is no one ever reacts until it happens to them, and then it's too late." She also recorded "I'll Fight," the theme song for *RBG,* an admiring documentary about the Supreme Court justice and liberal patron saint Ruth Bader Ginsburg.

Jennifer ended her relationship with Otunga in 2017, but through music, activism, and her son, she has found ways to move forward and keep hope alive. Hers is no longer a Cinderella story—she has fought to survive.

# MOTHER MARY

Christianity's Holy Mother teaches us to expect miracles, but also serves as a model of faith in the darkest of times. As a Christian herself who grew up singing in church, Jennifer Hudson embodies Mary's spirit. Jennifer has maintained faith in the good of the world through extraordinary circumstances, including losing several family members in a senseless, violent crime. She also thanked God for her miraculous—and well-deserved—Oscar win for her first movie role. She has spoken out about gun violence, but she has always maintained a hopeful view of humanity. Mary herself experienced the ultimate miracle when she gave birth to Jesus Christ. She also experienced the ultimate tragedy when she watched her son being persecuted, but she witnessed his resurrection, too. Jennifer's life and career demonstrate the ultimate highs and terrible lows of humanity, and the value in maintaining faith throughout.

## Invoke Jennifer for

Believing in miracles

Surviving unexpected difficulties

Seeing past momentary defeat

## How to channel Jennifer's goddess energy

Go for a long shot—a big audition, promotion, job, or anything you dream of but think is out of reach. You may not get it, but you will learn something from the process and may surprise yourself. (Or you may come in seventh place, then go on to win an Oscar.)

Find a specific political cause you believe in and do something concrete to work for it.

## JOURNAL RIFFS

What is the best thing you can think of that could happen to you right now that's at least a little within your control? (In other words, think writing a book, not winning the lottery.) What three steps can start you on your way?

If you achieved your greatest dream, what would your next goals be? Write down five goals that are beyond your wildest dreams.

## power songs

"Burden Down"

"Love You I Do"

"And I Am Telling You I'm Not Going"

"I Am Changing"

"Spotlight"

"Giving Myself"

"Think Like a Man"

"I Can't Describe (The Way I Feel)"

"Hallelujah"

"It's All Over"

# JENNIFER LOPEZ

## Goddess of Good Fortune

*Jennifer Lopez* devised a trick for getting over her insecurities: she wore a diamond ring that spelled out "I LOVE ME."

Regular folk may scoff at the idea of Jennifer Lopez, regarded as one of the most beautiful women in show business—and thus the world—needing such a reminder. But the size 6 singer-actress-mogul—size 4 in a serious workout phase, size 8 after the holidays, by her own account—spends a lot of her time surrounded by size 0 actresses and six-foot-tall models. In that light, she feels pretty "regular." And so she struggles.

She herself could see how ridiculous her ring therapy might have seemed, but by her forties, she had learned she needed it. "If you don't love yourself, you can't love anybody else," she told *Vogue*. "And I think as women we really forget that. All we want is to be happy, to feel secure, to feel understood. But you can't look for somebody else to

do that for you. You think about it: Oh, yeah, of course I care about myself. Of course I have good self-esteem. But when you really take a good look, you are not treating yourself like someone who does. And when you let people treat you in a way that you don't want to be treated, it's not their fault. It's yours."

The woman knows what she's talking about, especially when it comes to relationship ups and downs. Since her first high-profile romance with Sean "Puff Daddy" Combs from 1999 to 2001, Jennifer has notched an engagement to and breakup with actor Ben Affleck as well as a marriage to and divorce from fellow singer Marc Anthony, all under the watchful eye of judgmental gossipmongers, before ending up in what appears to be the most enviable of starry matches with baseball legend Alex Rodriguez.

In recent years, Jennifer and Alex have embodied #relationshipgoals, whether he was recording her on his phone as she performed at the 2018 MTV Video Music Awards, or they were posting Instagram photos of their children—including her twins with Anthony, Emme and Max—commingling. And for all the barbed remarks thrown at Lopez's penchant for serial monogamy, she has come out of it looking good, often photographed being friendly with exes Combs and Anthony.

"For me, the relationship journey has been very up and down," she told *Harper's Bazaar* in 2019. "But it didn't have to do with anyone else but me—it was about me figuring out me."

As her new philosophy manifested in her life, media coverage followed suit, switching from mocking her mercurial romantic life to fawning over her seemingly flawless relationship with Rodriguez, as well as her ageless body. Her narratives had converged: as she approached fifty, her beauty, success, relationship, fitness, and drive made her an aspirational figure. In the age of Instagram, she could display this all to its best advantage, without the vicious 2000s tabloid culture to turn it against her.

Jennifer Lynn Lopez was born on July 24, 1969, in the Bronx, New York, to Puerto Rican Americans Guadalupe Rodriguez and David Lopez. Jennifer began dancing as a young girl, training in ballet, jazz, and flamenco. She worked as a backup dancer in 1991 for New Kids on the Block, during a period that included the group's performance at the American Music Awards. The same year, the TV show *In Living Color* hired her as one of its Fly Girl dancers after she had struck out at the same audition the previous season. She wanted to sing and act as well, and she landed her first feature film roles in 1995's *My Family* and *Money Train*. After a few other movie roles, including *Blood and Wine* with Jack Nicholson, came her breakthrough: as the star of the 1997 biopic *Selena*, about the Mexican American Tejano singer who was shot and killed by a friend and business associate at the height of her fame. Roles in the thrillers *Anaconda* and *U Turn* followed, and 1998's *Out of Sight*, a steamy crime comedy co-starring George Clooney, solidified her fame.

The next year she pivoted to music with her debut album, *On the 6,* the title a reference to the subway line that runs between Jennifer's Bronx neighborhood and Manhattan. The songs merged radio-friendly R&B with her Latin roots, and among them were a number of hits: "If You Had My Love," "Waiting for Tonight," "Feelin' So Good," and "Let's Get Loud." The album, a surprise commercial success, garnered good reviews as well. The *Los Angeles Times* praised her vocals, calling them "as seductively emotive as her work on screen." NME set up an instant rivalry, saying, "Mariah Carey's ongoing quest for cool has just been dealt a severe blow." Lopez's emergence along with Ricky Martin, Enrique Iglesias, and Marc Anthony also put Latin music in the American mainstream.

In 2000, she had a different kind of star-making moment: one driven by fashion. She showed up at the Grammy Awards with then-boyfriend Combs while wearing a green silk chiffon Versace dress with a plunging neckline. The look became instantly iconic and made her a sex symbol.

Her second album, *J.Lo,* came out in January 2001 and solidified her status as a musical superstar, while also giving her an enduring nickname (as well as a celebrity nickname form that would be reused approximately one trillion times over). The record built upon her debut's Latin-tinged R&B with hits such as "Play," "Love Don't Cost a Thing," "I'm Real," and "Ain't It Funny." Despite mixed critical reception, the album debuted at number 1 on the *Billboard* charts. It also made her an international star, becoming a hit in Canada, Germany, Greece, Spain, Poland, and the UK. *J.Lo*'s release came with the announcement that she'd broken up with Combs, with whom she'd gotten into an image-straining scrape with the law in 1999, when they were arrested fleeing the scene of a New York nightclub shootout with a gun in the trunk of their Lincoln Navigator. Jennifer wasn't charged, but the incident wasn't an ideal movie-star look. She soon married backup dancer Cris Judd, who'd appeared in her "Love Don't Cost a Thing" video.

Her next album, *This Is Me . . . Then*, dropped in November 2002, and though it went double-platinum, it represented a serious dip in sales from her first two, dropping from the high of 3.8 million in the United States for *J.Lo* to 2.6 million. Drama roiled around Jennifer at this time: she divorced Judd just months before *This Is Me*'s release to pursue one of Hollywood's highest-profile romances of all time with A-list actor Ben Affleck, whom she'd met when they costarred in the film *Gigli*. By the time the album was coming out, the two had become engaged after a whirlwind romance, complete with 6-carat pink diamond engagement ring. Jennifer leaned into the attention, admitting in interviews that Affleck had inspired a lot of the songs on her new record. She even dedicated the album to him, writing on the CD jacket, "You are my life . . . my sole inspiration for every lyric, every emotion, every bit of feeling on this record." Tracks include "Loving You,"

"I'm Glad," "The One," "Dear Ben," "All I Have," "You Belong to Me," and "Baby I Love U!"

*This Is Me* also spawned the monstrous hit—and Jennifer's next nickname—"Jenny from the Block." Its refrain concentrates Jennifer's essence down to a few pithy lines: "Used to have a little, now I have a lot / No matter where I go, I know where I came from." She would continue to insist, for years to come, musically and in interviews, that she was just a regular girl from the Bronx . . . who happened to be blinged out at the moment.

The video for "Jenny from the Block" amplifies this confounding tone. It stars Jennifer and Ben—once again Jennifer was a nickname pioneer, becoming half of the first celebrity couple portmanteau, Bennifer. They let us in on the heights of their paparazzi bait days, reenacting being photographed frolicking in bathing suits on a boat (he caresses her famous booty), pumping gas (they kiss behind a tabloid mag), and cavorting on a hotel balcony (she gifts him an expensive watch). Two extraordinary sequences encapsulate this era of Jennifer's career: In the first, she's dressed in nothing but a short, white furry coat open at the front, silver panties, a medallion necklace, and hoop earrings at a photo shoot as she sings, "Put God first / Then can't forget to stay real / To me it's like breathing." In the second, two and a half minutes in, she breaks from "Jenny from the Block" for grainy footage of her looking casual in a white crop top and black track pants while jamming with a band on another track from the album, "Loving You"—a confident move from a celebrity at her peak who might imagine this as a grounded look at her going to work.

It all too soon came crashing down. Bennifer postponed, then canceled, their September 2003 wedding. They announced their breakup in early 2004. Jennifer reconnected with fellow singer Marc Anthony, with whom she'd performed a duet for *On the 6*. They married months later.

Jennifer's next album, *Rebirth*, came out the following year and signaled a necessary period of regrouping. It sold 745,000 copies in the United States, less than a third of what *This Is Me* sold. But that didn't matter. The album, she said, represented a new version of herself, an attempt to move past the "J.Lo" diva persona. It produced one memorable single, "Get Right," but wouldn't enter the pantheon of Jennifer's greatest hits.

But a low point inevitably gives way to an upward trajectory. Jennifer remained married to Anthony for seven years and gave birth to their twins in 2008. She replaced Ellen DeGeneres on the judging panel of the talent contest *American Idol* in 2011, which allowed her to display her warmth and charisma to a national audience twice a week—a move recognized as a reviving force in her career. That year, after separating from Anthony, she began dating backup dancer Casper Smart. She put out a new album, *Love?*, the same year. The breakout single, "On the Floor," debuted with its video on *Idol*. It featured a slight variation on her sound, incorporating the electro-pop Lady Gaga had made safe for radio, to great effect. The *Los Angeles Times* called the club-ready beat and catchy melody "vintage J.Lo."

Jennifer's 2014 album, *A.K.A.*, gave us a mixed bag: "I Luh Ya Papi" is an underrated experimental track, a love-it-or-hate-it combination of synth beats, hip-hop talk-singing, and a Bronx-tinged delivery few people besides Jennifer could pull off. "Booty" got far more attention for the obvious reasons, including an original version featuring Pitbull and a remix featuring Iggy Azalea rapping about her own derriere: "The last time the world seen a booty this good, it was on Jenny from the Block."

In many ways, Jennifer has transcended the mundanity of chart success or lack thereof. She has become arguably the most powerful Hispanic performer in Hollywood. Her parallel careers in movies and music made her stronger; the Pop Star Goddess Jennifer Lopez is more than the sum of her parts. In fact, one of her greatest powers is combining the relatable Jenny from the Block—despite that video, she somehow convinced us anyway—with the untouchable star who is dancing, acting, and singing right into her fifties and beyond, looking flawless the whole way. The 2001 rom-com *The Wedding Planner* and 2018's *Second Act* didn't make her a star. Neither did "Love Don't Cost a Thing" nor "Booty," nor her relationships with Ben Affleck and Alex Rodriguez.

What made her a star is that she is Jennifer Lopez, and no matter what she does, we're interested.

## Jennifer's Ancient Goddess Sister
# LAKSHMI

Lakshmi represents abundance, just as Jennifer Lopez does. Jennifer wants us to see she's "real" because she wants us to see that good fortune is just as possible for us as it is for her. As misguided as this posturing may have seemed, it comes from a genuine place (in case you didn't hear the first twenty-seven trillion times, the Bronx). One mantra calls Lakshmi the "giver of . . . worldly enjoyment and liberation." Lakshmi was invoked in ancient India for fame and prosperity; J.Lo has experienced the heights of both, with their positive and dark sides. A Tantric hymn asks of Lakshmi: "O Mother / Deeply embedded / Is my fear, my insecurity. / Have mercy, O Mother, on my wretched state. / Uproot it / With the joy that arises from your sweet and compassionate glance." Jennifer's "I LOVE ME" ring, if placed on your finger, could have the same effect. Perhaps even just thinking about it could.

## Invoke Jennifer for

Getting over insecurity

Making peace with your exes

Figuring yourself out

Maintaining your health

Feeling beautiful

Embracing success

Pursuing multiple interests

## How to channel Jennifer's goddess energy

Give yourself a nickname that embodies the qualities
you want to have right now.

Buy yourself your equivalent of bling, within your price range,
whether it's a costume-jewelry ring, a diamond,
a great body scrub, or a sumptuous sweater.

Meditate on the mantra "I love me."

## JOURNAL RIFFS

What do you love most about yourself?

How could you make peace with your exes, even if from a distance?
What blessings could you send them?

## power songs

"Booty"

"Jenny from the
Block"

"Love Don't Cost a
Thing"

"Ain't It Funny"

"Dinero"

"I Luh Ya Papi"

"I'm Real"

"Play"

"On the Floor"

"I'm into You"

"Waiting for Tonight"

"Feelin' So Good"

"Get Right"

# KACEY MUSGRAVES

## Goddess of the Unconventional

*Kacey Musgraves* broke through to mainstream musical success in a way no one has ever done before: by writing a catchy song with a classic country sound and lyrics espousing the joys of marijuana and same-sex love. With that 2013 song, "Follow Your Arrow," she joined the pantheon of defiant country queens—Dolly Parton with her feminist anthems "Dumb Blonde" and "Just Because I'm a Woman"; Loretta Lynn with her ode to the power of birth control, "The Pill"; the Dixie Chicks with their revenge fantasy, "Goodbye Earl."

Even so, Kacey staged her rebellion in a fresh way with "Follow Your Arrow," which, as Jewly Hight wrote for NPR, "felt like a low-key intervention in countrified attitudes, particularly because there was no indignation to her performance. She shrugged off judgmental perceptions of a person's sex life, choice of partner and drinking and smoking habits as though they were nothing to get worked up about."

The album that included "Follow Your Arrow," *Same Trailer Different Park*, didn't stop at just one shock for conservative country music. In "Merry Go 'Round," she takes aim at the conventional march toward matrimony: "We get bored so we get married / And just like dust we settle in this town." The track "It Is What It Is" details a no-strings-attached sexual relationship. "My grandma calls this 'the slut song,'" Kacey often tells audiences.

This stealth progressiveness has become the singer-songwriter's signature: she looks like a standard country sweetheart, with long, dark hair and, at times, a penchant for country kitsch like rhinestones, fringe, and Daisy Dukes. But listen closely, and you'll hear messages like: "Kiss lots of boys / Or kiss lots of girls / If that's something you're into." As she told *Billboard*, "There's a freedom in putting yourself out there from day one, never trying to fit someone else's mold."

The approach has won her acclaim, awards, and a large and passionate fan base. But it has kept her off country radio for much of her career. Though she isn't the only woman in country music battling overt sexism, she has become emblematic of the problem—and a vocal critic of the industry. "Somehow this tiny, impactful singer registers as something of a weirdo around the Nashville mainstream-country scene," Craig Jenkins wrote on Vulture. "It's a demure and conservative community, the kind that gasps at a low-cut neckline on an award-show red carpet and rattles sabers all night when

Beyoncé and the Dixie Chicks sing a song together on national television."

Kacey was born on August 21, 1988, in the East Texas town of Golden. She was living in Texas's liberal enclave, Austin, when she signed with independent label Triple Pop in 2008. The label released an EP of her country takes on two pop songs, OneRepublic's "Apologize" and Miley Cyrus's "See You Again." Major label Mercury Nashville picked her up and released her 2012 debut single, "Merry Go 'Round," which ended up on *Same Trailer Different Park* when the full album dropped the following year. Kacey didn't hide her liberal proclivities; she happily performed "Follow Your Arrow" on NPR to celebrate the U.S. Supreme Court's 2015 decision legalizing same-sex marriage nationwide.

She followed *Same Trailer Different Park* with the similar-sounding *Pageant Material* in 2015 and built on her success: the album debuted at number 1 on *Billboard*'s Top Country Albums chart. But her personal life took a turn soon afterward: she met her future husband, fellow singer-songwriter Ruston Kelly, in the most Nashville way possible in March 2016—at the Bluebird Café after Kelly performed. They married in October 2017.

Inspired by love (and some acid trips), she began writing songs for her 2018 crossover success, *Golden Hour*—a trippy, dancey, poppy, but also still country record recognized for its genre-busting qualities. "I'm coming off getting married and being in this golden hour of my personal life, where all these things are finally coming to fruition," she told *Entertainment Weekly*. "I found myself inspired to write about this person and all these things he brought out in me that weren't there before."

The idea for the opening track, "Slow Burn," came to her during an LSD trip. And once again, she refused to apologize, this time for her drug-assisted methods or for the turn in her sound. "If you hear that song and you don't like it, you're not going to like the rest of this record, so stop listening, basically," she told the *New York Times*.

Music critics did not want to stop listening—they loved it. Stephen Thomas Erlewine wrote at AllMusic that *Golden Hour* was "warm and enveloping, pitched halfway between heartbreak and healing—but [it] lingers in the mind because the songs are so sharp, buttressed by long, loping melodies and Musgraves' affectless soul baring." The website Wide Open Country praised the record's "cosmic femininity." Jenkins wrote for Vulture, "*Golden Hour* makes mincemeat of both the trepidation about the quality of country women's art and the fuss about them crossing over." It won the Country Music Association's Album of the Year award and several Grammys, including Album of the Year. To promote it, Kacey went on tour with former boy bander Harry Styles, a team-up that would have seemed baffling a year earlier but felt right because of Styles's own transformation into a groovy, throwback rocker in the 1970s mold.

Kacey's career so far shows us the magic that can happen when you mix elements that don't belong together: country and progressive thinking, country and LSD, country and dance. Even country and drag: in 2019 she was a guest judge on *RuPaul's Drag Race All Stars* and brought the winners onstage to perform with her at her Los Angeles tour stop. "As country's mainstream has become more distanced from its heritage, Ms. Musgraves has somehow become both the keeper of the genre's old rules and also its leading internal dissenter," Jon Caramanica wrote in the *New York Times*.

As a Pop Star Goddess, Kacey matches anyone whose spirit animal is a butterfly, who likes a little CBD oil in her tea or goes on ayahuasca retreats. As is true for many Pop Star Goddesses, her style, beauty, and zero-fucks attitude, as well as her outspoken activism, have made her a queer idol. She represents optimism, freedom, and peace. But she isn't above a little (or a lot of) sparkle and glamour. She has said that if she weren't a singer-songwriter she'd like to be a yoga teacher. She decorates her trailer with uplifting touches like tiny pink roses, white geodes, and Jenni Kayne candles. Her lyrics tell us one thing above all others: we're all flawed, and that's okay.

## Kacey's Ancient Goddess Sister
# LIBERTAS

Libertas is the Roman goddess of freedom, of liberty. A simple, straightforward goddess, she represents a quality Romans treasured. (Other such gods and goddesses honored hope, piety, and courage.) She served as inspiration for the fledgling nation of America: Paul Revere depicted her on an obelisk celebrating the repeal of the Stamp Act; Thomas Paine referenced her in his poem "Liberty Tree" as "the goddess of liberty." The female symbol of the subsequent French Revolution, Marianne, was also derived from Libertas. French sculptor Frédéric-Auguste Bartholdi used her as the model for the Statue of Liberty, which commemorated France and America's friendship and mutual commitment to freedom in the late nineteenth century. France gave the Statue of Liberty, originally called "Liberty Enlightening the World," to the United States for its one hundredth birthday.

The spirit of Libertas imbues Kacey Musgraves, from her outspoken lyrics to her cross-genre pollination. She values her own freedom and advocates for others' freedom as well. She comes from the South, where American patriotism runs deep, and her career embodies the American Dream: she has risen from a tiny town to chart-topping success by dint of her hard work and talent.

## Invoke Kacey for

Connecting with your spirit

Replenishing your energy

Expressing yourself any damn way you please

## How to channel Kacey's goddess energy

Meditate for a natural high.

Speak up for others.

Practice yoga.

Beautify your space with flowers, crystals, or candles.

Accept your own flaws and the flaws of others.

Celebrate and advocate for true freedom for all.

Indulge in comfort at home with cozy sweatshirts and pajama pants or glam up for going out in makeup, heels, jewelry, and sparkle.

## JOURNAL RIFFS

What gives you hope for the future?

What freedoms mean the most to you?

What message do you want your life to send to the world?

## power songs

"Slow Burn"

"Butterflies"

"Oh, What a World"

"Wonder Woman"

"High Horse"

"Rainbow"

"See You Again"

"Pageant Material"

"Biscuits"

"Family Is Family"

"Merry Go 'Round"

"Blowin' Smoke"

"The Trailer Song"

"Dime Store Cowgirl"

"Follow Your Arrow"

## Goddess of Domination

*Katy Perry* appears on *Sesame Street* wearing a minidress with a yellow bodice that seems strapless but is anchored by a sheer top that runs up to her shoulder line. A veil with three big, fluffy flowers at the crown sits atop her head as she greets the red puppet character Elmo and asks, "Are you ready to play dress-up?"

When Elmo skitters away, she launches into a kiddie version of her song "Hot n Cold": "You're up then you're down, you're running around / You're fast then you're slow, you stop then you go." This adorable bit fits perfectly in the *Sesame Street* tradition of hip guest stars appearing in kid-friendly, light parodies of themselves. But this one never aired: after the segment debuted online, enough parents complained about Katy's "revealing" outfit, according to *Time*, to get it pulled from the broadcast.

She became the queen of pop radio, churning out hit after hit, by walking this exact line, between cute and provocative, cartoonish and sexy, with a truckload of earworms in tow to make you forget these contradictions. But her toggling has also gotten her in trouble with more than *Sesame Street* parents. Her 2017 album, *Witness,* which she described as "purposeful pop," felt like empty pandering to a hyperpoliticized moment. She's appropriated other cultures' looks for videos (though she's hardly the only Pop Star Goddess to do so) and stumbled through a years-long feud with Taylor Swift (also not Taylor's best look), only recently resolved.

Perhaps what makes Katy different is that she cleverly built "problematic" right into her pop star persona. Her 2008 breakthrough smash, "I Kissed a Girl," felt less-than-acceptable in its time, much less as it has aged. She was knowingly playing to the girl-on-girl-for-men's-sake trope, protesting a little too much with the oft-repeated disclaimer of the chorus: "Hope my boyfriend don't mind it." The song incurred entertaining backlash from all sides and came out a winner. It worked. Her major-label debut album, *One of the Boys*—a great pop-rock record, front-to-back—coasted on the massive success of "I Kissed a Girl" and the follow-up single she parodied in her *Sesame Street* appearance, "Hot n Cold."

What also makes Katy different is that she has notched an incredible stream of hits, putting up exceptional stats

144  even among the upper echelon of Pop Star Goddesses.

Playing up her sex appeal didn't hurt: *GQ* described her as a "full-on male fantasy" and *Elle Canada* described her body "as though sketched by a teenage boy." But she backed up her sex symbol status with serious pop song magic. Her 2010 record, *Teenage Dream*, tripled down on the bombast of "I Kissed a Girl" and became the second album in history to score five number 1 hits, after Michael Jackson's *Bad* in 1987. Along the way, she maybe, almost, let fans glimpse the authentic Katy. In the 2012 documentary *Katy Perry: Part of Me* (note: not titled *All of Me*), she chronicles her difficulties touring the world in 2011 while trying to make married life with comedian Russell Brand work; by the end of the film, he has texted her that he's filing for divorce. The film closes with her breakup anthem, "Part of Me," and, well, I dare you not to cry. The documentary was also a box office hit.

And at the exact same time that Katy's feud with Taylor—apparently a squabble over dancers—went public, Katy championed a different fellow Pop Star Goddess, Kacey Musgraves. The two performed together in a 2014 episode of CMT's series *Crossroads* and gave some adorable interviews together to promote it. "I love all her songs, but for some reason 'Keep It to Yourself' is particularly heartfelt for me," Katy said. "When we do that song on *Crossroads*, I'm not going to do anything besides go cry in the corner."

In short, Katy Perry has her complications and contradictions, but she is foremost a star. She has dominated her

business. And no matter what happens for the rest of her career, that fact remains.

Katy Perry was born in Santa Barbara, California, on October 25, 1984, as Katheryn Elizabeth Hudson, to pastors Keith and Mary Hudson. She had a religious and restricted childhood in which she sang in the church choir and wasn't allowed to listen to secular music or watch much television. She did, however, take voice lessons. The experience stimulated her ambitions, prompting her to complete her GED at age fifteen so she could leave Dos Pueblos High School and pursue a music career.

She first released a Christian pop record under her birth name, Katy Hudson, in 2001. She hoped to be as successful as gospel-pop crossover artist Amy Grant, but the album fizzled.

When Katy decided to switch to mainstream pop instead, she moved to Los Angeles. She suffered a few broken record deals before she hit gold with Capitol Records, for whom she and producer Dr. Luke wrote "I Kissed a Girl." She changed her name (using her mom's maiden name) to avoid confusion with actress Kate Hudson and never looked back.

Katy admitted to questioning her hit-making abilities: "When I am in between records, sometimes I doubt myself. I'll be like 'Did I just get lucky, or did I mass-manipulate the world into thinking that seven songs were worth a number-one position?'" She proved those abilities again in 2013, scoring even with the slightly toned-down *Prism*, boosted by hits such as "Roar" and "Dark Horse."

Katy was counted among the most listened-to acts of 2014 on the streaming service Spotify. She recorded the anthem for the 2016 Summer Olympics, "Rise." She became the only artist ever to have three songs certified diamond (the rare designation higher than platinum) as of 2017: "Roar," "Dark Horse," and "Firework." She was named the highest-earning female artist of 2018 by *Forbes*.

She is a star for the masses. If you go to one of her concerts, she's likely to play all her biggest hits and to reassure the crowd that they're all coming. She will put on a huge show with lavish costumes and sets, all the crowd-pleasers. She is a Big Pop Star, and she's not afraid to admit it.

KATY PERRY

# BHUVANESHWARI

Hinduism's Bhuvaneshwari is described in Sally Kempton's *Awakening Shakti* as the "goddess of infinite space, she whose body is the world." Katy Perry has united millions through her music, dominating the charts more than even the biggest of her fellow goddesses. She draws riches with the power of her creativity, which is not as easy as she makes it look. Of course, this approach includes a downside: when she fills the large space she occupies in our culture with less-than-inspiring material, it produces an extra drag on the collective energy. In other words, we notice more when an album like *Witness* is void of inspiration. Not every song or album must pulse with meaning; there is value in moving people to dance or feel a little lighter. Taking up such a large cultural space brings power and its responsibility. Katy has that power.

## Invoke Katy for

Dominating your profession

Getting attention

Enduring rejection on the way to success

Surpassing your goals

Appealing to the masses without apology

## How to channel Katy's goddess energy

Make a plan for starting your own business or for whatever your biggest professional goals are.

Research how much the highest-paid people in your field make and how to get there yourself.

Champion other women in your industry or community.

## JOURNAL RIFFS

What do you most want to dominate? How can you do it?

What would the cartoon character version of you look like?

If you were famous, what would you be most likely to do that would incur backlash?

## power songs

"Swish Swish"

"Firework"

"Teenage Dream"

"Rise"

"California Gurls"

"I Kissed a Girl"

"One of the Boys"

"Waking Up in Vegas"

"Ur So Gay"

"Hot n Cold"

"I'm Still Breathing"

"Roar"

"Dark Horse"

"Chained to the Rhythm"

# KELLY CLARKSON

## Goddess of Getting Real

*In 2002,* Kelly Clarkson stood before three judges on a new reality TV show, *American Idol*: pop superstar Paula Abdul, producer Simon Cowell, and musician Randy Jackson. The twenty-year-old Texan, clad in a frayed, strapless top she'd made herself out of an old pair of acid-wash jeans, had just finished belting out a cappella renditions of Etta James's "At Last" and Madonna's "Express Yourself" and was awaiting judgment.

Most of us, even the truly talented among us, would shake with nerves in such a scenario. Instead, Kelly appeared unfazed as she joked with the judges. Jackson mentioned he'd worked with Madonna on her song. "I can't help it if I'm famous, man," Jackson said as his fellow judges laughed. "I love me."

"That's cool," Kelly replied. "You should be a star. I think you should try out. Look, I'll take your place."

And just like that, she was swapping places with Jackson, sitting comfortably next to one of her idols, Abdul, as Jackson warbled a weak rendition of R. Kelly's "I Believe I Can Fly."

Continuing to play along straight through offering a verdict on his performance, Kelly mockingly approved and said he was fit for the next round of the show: "It's the personality, man. You're gonna go."

When the judges told her the obvious—she was the one going to Hollywood—she looked psyched but not surprised. "Score," she said, as if she just got the job she'd hoped for at the mall food court.

Her brown hair streaked with blond highlights, she did look like a cute girl you'd find working at your local mall, but, as we'd see throughout that season of *Idol*, she sang Aretha Franklin and the big band classic "Stuff Like That There" with a conviction and power that should never have happened on American TV's first major talent competition show since *Star Search*. The universe must have meant for *American Idol* to be the dominant television hit of the 2000s. Nothing else makes sense.

Kelly won that first season of *Idol* in 2002, and she has remained successful ever since. She has done this in spite of—or, more likely, because of—her commitment to realness. She posts online videos of herself whiffing on major notes while recording her albums. She tweets her incredulity when someone like Weezer's Rivers Cuomo praises her most recent record. She does live video chats with fans while drinking red wine.

Kelly Clarkson was born in Texas on April 24, 1982. She has since become known for her massive vocals as well as her long, flowing, golden hair extensions (another piece of Hollywood trickery she's quick to cop to in interviews), easy smile, fluctuating weight (for which she refuses to apologize), and sparkly outfits. She and her husband live on a farm just outside Nashville with chickens, honeybees, and an orchard—an enviable but low-key life.

The pop singer has a vivacious personality, but she is most known for her unapologetic self-expression. She remains, for her part, mystified by the idea that this makes her special: "I always laugh at the concept that people are like, 'We just love what you say; that's why we love you,' and I'm like, 'Why is everyone not like that?' That's what boggles my mind. Why would you *not* say what you want to say?"

She also gets frustrated by people who try to silence her from expressing political opinions. She said in an interview, "I always hate when people bring up, 'Oh, you're a celebrity, you shouldn't have an opinion.' . . . I'm not just that. I'm a mother, I'm a daughter, I'm a woman." Instead of letting such sentiment subdue her, she has voiced plenty of her controversial opinions. She has tweeted about violence at a white supremacist demonstration in Charlottesville, Virginia; NFL players' right to protest by kneeling during the national anthem; and her support for presidential candidate Hillary Clinton. (Clinton later returned the favor in her book *What Happened*, citing Kelly's song

"Stronger," along with Nietzsche, as the source for the quote, "That which does not kill us makes us stronger." Clarkson's Twitter response: "Yaaaasssss! #philosopher goals.") When Kelly hosted the 2018 Billboard Music Awards, she declined to do a standard moment of silence for the most recent of many deadly mass shootings at U.S. schools. Instead, she said, "I'm so sick of 'moment of silence.' It's not working. So why don't we not do a moment of silence? Why don't we do a moment of action? Why don't we do a moment of change?"

When it comes to talking about her diet and exercise, she stays equally real. No wise and sanguine lifestyle advice here. "I started doing yoga and it always looks like simple stretching," she said. "That is a lie, my friend. It is hard." On having four kids, she said, "Wine is necessary." Even when she did lose some weight, she joked, "I have to shout out my whole glam squad. I literally hired Harry Potter and SPANX; it's all like a sausage."

She also doesn't mind sharing her more difficult, personal feelings, like the hurt she experienced when her father disappeared from her life after her parents' divorce when she was six. "Watching my husband love on his daughter all the time, you know, go to her events and just be there and, like, be present is hard to watch but beautiful to watch," she told *Idol* host Ryan Seacrest in an interview. She channeled that pain into several hit songs, such as "Because of You" and "Piece by Piece," which she performed during a 2016 appearance on *Idol* at eight months pregnant and broke down in tears. Judges Keith Urban and Jennifer Lopez cried along with her.

"You can try your hardest to salvage relationships—and I did—but at the end of the day, if you keep getting hurt by someone because they just don't know how to properly love people, it's not worth it," she said. "It's not worth the strain in your heart and it starts to bleed into your other relationships and it becomes super dysfunctional."

She has gotten most vocal about the creative sacrifices she was forced to make after winning *Idol*. She called the first four years of her post-*Idol* career "almost total crap." (The cringe-worthy movie featuring her and runner-up Justin Guarini, 2003's *From Justin to Kelly*, perhaps best encapsulates this phenomenon.) She bickered with Clive Davis, the chair and CEO of her record label, RCA Music Group, over his attempts to change her 2007 record, *My December.* "I did call my mom at some point, and I was just like, you know what, this is just not fun," she told the *New York Times.* "I had fun waitressing. I had fun being a promo girl for Red Bull. I had fun working at Papa John's. And this is my dream, and this is not fun."

After she finished out the RCA contract that came as part of her *Idol* prize, she signed instead with Atlantic Records. Her first Atlantic release, 2017's *Meaning of Life*, triumphed artistically. "It's just the first record I've made that I didn't call my mother, wanting to quit," Kelly said. "And I'm not a baby, y'all. I'm strong. There are songs about it! I'm a very powerful, confident woman, but at the same time, you just feel beaten down."

One of the album's standout tracks, "Whole Lotta Woman," celebrates her very essence. "It took me a while to fall in love because I am a whole lot of woman—I have a big personality, I'm a grown-ass woman that can pay her bills, and I make a lot of money," she said to *Rolling Stone*, explaining the song's origins. "That's intimidating." The song also addresses the conversation about weight that has followed her—like most female stars—for her entire career. "Even when I was on *Idol,* it was a discussion," she said. "So it was fun to write a song that said, 'Yeah, you're right, I *am* a whole lot of woman, and it's okay. I came with a brain, and I came with drive and passion and sensuality, and these things that are awesome. If you can't handle it, that's totally cool, but you're not tall enough to ride this ride, move along. It's fine.'"

As a coach on the *Idol*-like singing competition *The Voice* in 2018, she advised her victorious mentee, Brynn Cartelli, not to make the same mistakes she did. "It's not worth it," she said, "unless you're having a good time." She gives her kids similarly hard-earned advice: "You stand up for yourself."

## Kelly's Ancient Goddess Sister
# AMATERASU

This deity of the Japanese Shinto faith—the sun goddess—did not suffer fools. Amaterasu got into a fight with her brother, Susanoo (the god of storms and the sea), when he threw a flayed horse into her weaving hall (as one does). Her reaction: holing up in a cave and bringing an age of darkness onto the world, much like Queen Elsa's ice storm in *Frozen*. She eventually came out of the cave and made peace with Susanoo, who offered her a legendary sword as a reconciliation gift. Think of Clarkson's newest record deal and *Meaning of Life* as her sword.

## Invoke Kelly for

Expressing your truth
Owning your mistakes
Feeling good in your body just as it is

## How to channel Kelly's goddess energy

Fight for success, but on your own terms.
Don't worry (too much) about how you look.
Don't apologize for feeling damn good about yourself.

## JOURNAL RIFFS

What do you want to change in the world, and what action
can you take to do that?
What's one thing you beat yourself up about that you could let go of?
What gives you joy, and how can you do more of it?
What would happen if you always said what you meant?

## power songs

"Mr. Know It All"
"Don't Let Me Stop
   You"
"Whole Lotta
   Woman"
"Breakaway"
"Stronger"

"Walk Away"
"Since U Been Gone"
"Dark Side"
"I Don't Think About
   You"
"Move You"
"I Want You"

"Medicine"
"I Do Not Hook Up"
"Miss Independent"
"Go High"
"Because of You"

# KESHA

## Goddess of Asking for What You Need

*At Timberline* Knolls, a women's treatment center in suburban Lemont, Illinois, Kesha had to beg for a small, battery-operated keyboard. She had checked in earlier that year, 2014, for help with an eating disorder. She wanted to get better, but she was desperate to write songs. So a friend brought her the tiny instrument. At first the staff balked. She couldn't have anything that could be used to attempt suicide, like anything with a power cord, they explained.

"I respect all of that, but please let me have a keyboard or my brain's going to explode," she later recalled saying. "My head has all these song ideas in it, and I just really need to play an instrument." After some negotiation, the staff let her keep it. She ended up recording fourteen songs while she was there.

After she completed the residential program, Kesha made another life-changing decision: in October of that same year, she sued the Svengali producer who had guided her hit-making career thus far, Dr. Luke—legal name Lukasz Sebastian Gottwald—who had an impressive résumé full of massive pop singles such as Kelly Clarkson's

"Since U Been Gone," Pink's "U + Ur Hand," Katy Perry's "I Kissed a Girl," and Miley Cyrus's "Party in the U.S.A."

Kesha's suit accused Dr. Luke of sexual assault and battery, sexual harassment, gender violence, emotional abuse, and violation of California business practices during their decade of working together. She claimed he had raped her in his hotel room in 2005 after they attended a party together for heiress Nicky Hilton's birthday. Kesha alleged Dr. Luke gave her GHB, the "date rape drug" (which he referred to at the time as "sober pills"), took her back to his hotel room, and assaulted her while she was unconscious. Kesha also alleged he had verbally bullied her about her weight, sparking her eating disorder. (She later publicly released emails she said were from Dr. Luke to back up the latter claim, which included him saying, "A-list songwriters and producers are reluctant to give Kesha their songs because of her weight.")

But her legal actions were stymied, and Dr. Luke has denied all the accusations. In fact, he countersued Kesha and her mother, Pebe Sebert, claiming their "false and shocking" accusations surrounding her suit amounted to extortion. His suit said, "Kesha's repudiation of this contractual relationship, and her and her mother's ongoing campaign to extort a release by tarnishing Gottwald's reputation, has caused damage" to Dr. Luke's business.

In April 2016, a New York judge dismissed Kesha's case seeking to be released from her contract and claiming sexual assault, sexual harassment, and gender violence. As

the legal wrangling dragged on, Kesha posted on Instagram that Dr. Luke had agreed to free her from her contract if she would recant her abuse accusations. She said
she had declined, because she "would rather let the truth
ruin my career than lie for a monster ever again."

In August 2016, she dropped her Los Angeles case accusing Dr. Luke of sexual abuse. She wrote on Facebook at
the time: "I need to get my music out. I have so much to
say. This lawsuit is so heavy on my once free spirit, and I
can only pray to one day feel that happiness again."

Still, her determination to speak out about abuse by
a powerful man—one who had been a part of her first
two albums' massive success—struck a nerve. Twenty
months before a litany of sexual assault and harassment
allegations against movie producer Harvey Weinstein
spawned the #MeToo movement, celebrities were voicing
their support for Kesha on social media with the hashtag
#FreeKesha. "There are people all around the world who
love you @KeshaRose," Lady Gaga tweeted. "Standing
with @KeshaRose during this traumatic, deeply unfair
time," Lorde tweeted. "Disgusted by anyone in power positions abusing their authority," Halsey tweeted. "Frus-
trating to see women come forward with their past only to
be shot down, not believed & disrespected for their bravery in taking action," Demi Lovato tweeted. Taylor Swift
donated $250,000 to help Kesha pursue her case. Other
celebrity women supporting Kesha included Anne Hatha-
way, Lena Dunham, Reese Witherspoon, Adele, Ariana

Grande, Janelle Monáe, Iggy Azalea, Sara Bareilles, and Mariska Hargitay. Fans backed Kesha's cause, too, even protesting outside the Sony Records offices in New York City.

Amid the public uproar, Dr. Luke was forced to step down as CEO of Kemosabe Records.

Contractual arrangements meant he still stood to profit from Kesha's next release. But the battle transformed her into a symbol of empowerment, so much so that she provided "Here Comes the Change," the theme song for the film *On the Basis of Sex,* a biopic about another totem of empowerment, Supreme Court Justice Ruth Bader Ginsburg.

Kesha Rose Sebert was born on March 1, 1987, in Los Angeles. During her childhood, she, her brother, and her mother, Pebe, moved to Nashville, where Pebe worked as a songwriter whose output included Dolly Parton's 1980 hit "Old Flames Can't Hold a Candle to You." It soon became apparent that Kesha got Pebe's songwriting gene. She started recording demos while still in high school in Nashville. Her big break came when one of them got to Dr. Luke in 2005. At eighteen, Kesha moved to Los Angeles and signed with his label, Kemosabe, and his publishing company, Prescription Songs, as a writer. In 2009, she found herself on mainstream radio for the first time, as the featured vocalist on Flo Rida's hit "Right Round," which Dr. Luke produced.

Her debut studio album, *Animal,* came out on January 1, 2010, after seven years of work and more than two

hundred songs written. She cultivated a party-girl image with messy hair, smeared mascara, and torn tights, and spelled her name in a stylized way like a rapper: Ke$ha. About the title of the record, Kesha said, "I named it that because I want people to lose it when they listen to my record and go to the animal part of themselves that they suppress." It included a slew of 1980s pop-influenced party tracks such as "Boots & Boys," "Your Love Is My Drug," and "Party at a Rich Dude's House."

The first single, "Tik Tok," became the bestselling single of 2010. The opening quatrain proved an instant classic: "Wake up in the morning feeling like P. Diddy / Grab my glasses, I'm out the door, I'm gonna hit this city / Before I leave, brush my teeth with a bottle of Jack."

In the next few years, she released the follow-up EP *Cannibal*, meant to capitalize on *Animal*'s success, and the party-happy, electronically driven *Warrior* in 2012. By this time, a *New Yorker* profile of Dr. Luke described his working relationship with Kesha as "strained" because she wanted to record more rock-influenced songs, rather than the party pop that had made her famous. She also cowrote songs for several other artists, including Britney Spears (the showstopper "Till the World Ends") and Ariana Grande ("Pink Champagne").

But Kesha's bulimia treatment in 2014 and lawsuit against Dr. Luke marked a major turning point. In 2017, five years after *Warrior*, she released *Rainbow*—recorded at Kesha's own expense and written and produced without

Dr. Luke, but still on his label. She dropped the $ symbol from her name and the morning-after look, though she defended her former self in interviews, speaking of herself like one would refer to a younger sister.

*Rainbow* triumphed artistically and marked a departure for Kesha. It featured more rock and Americana and confessional lyrics, and guest performances by Eagles of Death Metal and Dolly Parton. The lead single, "Praying," had a not-so-coded message: "Told me that I was nothing without you / Oh, but after everything you've done / I can thank you for how strong I have become."

She wrote in the newsletter Lenny Letter about the song: "I have channeled my feelings of severe hopelessness and depression, I've overcome obstacles, and I have found strength in myself even when it felt out of reach. I've found what I had thought was an unobtainable place of peace. . . . 'Praying' was written about that moment when the sun starts peeking through the darkest storm clouds, creating the most beautiful rainbow. Once you realize that you will in fact be OK, you want to spread love and healing."

The album debuted at number 1 and resulted in a cathartic Grammy performance of "Praying" in 2018, as the #MeToo movement reached critical mass. Janelle Monáe introduced the performance, saying, "We come in peace, but we mean business." Kesha appeared to choke back tears through her delivery of the chorus as she was backed by a dozen or so women, all dressed in white, including Cyndi Lauper, Camila Cabello, Julia Michaels,

Andra Day, and Bebe Rexha. The women all embraced at the end.

The rest of Kesha's album proved equally significant, to listeners as well as to Kesha, who told the *Guardian* the songs were "truly from the inside of my guts." The record marked her return from a "really sad, lonely, dark place," she said. On *Good Morning America*, she said, "This album quite literally saved my life."

She wrote the song "Bastards" by herself on a guitar at 4 A.M. "because I don't understand why people are so fucking mean to each other," she said, "but I can't change it and writing is how I cope with everything." "Let 'Em Talk" tackles the same sentiment from the opposite direction: "It's kind of part of a running theme: basically it's about those same bastards that try to bring you down, but it's about not caring, letting go of control and letting them do whatever they're gonna do."

*USA Today* called another of the album's standout tracks, "Woman," "the feminist song of the summer" in 2017. Kesha underscored that sentiment with an essay about "Woman" for *Rolling Stone*: "I have always been a feminist, but for much of my life I felt like a little girl trying to figure things out," she wrote. "In the past few years, I have felt like a woman more than ever. I just feel the strength and awesomeness and power of being female. We hold the key to humanity."

## Kesha's Ancient Goddess Sister
# BRIGIT

Brigit urges us to stand firm as we speak up for what we believe. "Even in the face of fear, you can still stand up for your ideals and your truth," she urges in Doreen Virtue's *Goddess Guidance Oracle Cards*. "Be unwavering, and make your stand today!" Kesha manifests this kind of strength. She declared the most difficult of her truths to the world, accusing a powerful man of wrongdoing. She asked for what she deserved, which required lawyers, courts, and the testimony of other powerful people. Even if she didn't win in court, she served as a role model for other young women who have suffered similar fates and started a necessary public discussion that would eventually feed into the larger #MeToo movement. She also scored an artistic triumph, even if its circumstances were less than perfect. Kesha trusted her own truth, just like Brigit, a Celtic goddess who serves as the female counterpart to the warrior Archangel Michael. Brigit is celebrated on February 1, as spring approaches with more daylight—and hope for the future.

## Invoke Kesha for

Speaking out against abuses of power

Asking for what you need

Seeking help for mental and emotional problems

## How to channel Kesha's goddess energy

Make the project you want to make, even if it means financing it yourself and/or continuing to work a day job.

Get yourself your own version of a toy keyboard—a small investment in self-expression.

## JOURNAL RIFFS

What do you need most in your life right now?

How can you get it or ask for it?

Write a letter to the person you were ten years ago.

## power songs

"Tik Tok"
"Stephen"
"Party at a Rich
   Dude's House"
"Backstabber"
"Dinosaur"

"Boots & Boys"
"Bastards"
"Let 'Em Talk"
"Woman"
"Hymn"
"Praying"

"Learn to Let Go"
"Rainbow"
"Boots"
"Spaceship"
"We R Who We R"

## Goddess of Social Justice

*Lady Gaga* had used a "vomit artist" in outrageous live performances, had worn a dress (and matching hat) made of raw beef, had arrived at an award ceremony carried inside a giant plastic egg, and had covered herself in blood and set herself on fire onstage.

It all served the moments that counted. Because of her performance-art antics, she'd become an international superstar. So when, for instance, she spoke at a tribute to the victims of a mass shooting at a gay nightclub in Orlando, Florida, in 2016, she commanded the world's attention. In natural makeup and a black T-shirt, her blond hair tucked into a black baseball cap, she addressed a crowd in Los Angeles, her voice wavering: "This is an attack on humanity itself. This is an attack on everyone. . . . I hope you know that myself and so many are your allies. . . . You are not alone."

At this, Lady Gaga has become a master unlike any in

pop star history: she knows how to shock the world to attention with fashion and performance, and then channel that attention to the causes closest to her heart—LGBTQ equality above all others. Plenty of Pop Star Goddesses have enthusiastic gay followings; few (since Madonna) have taken up gay equality like Gaga.

Stefani Joanne Angelina Germanotta was born on March 28, 1986, in New York City. Raised Catholic, she grew up listening to Michael Jackson, Stevie Wonder, Queen, Pink Floyd, Mariah Carey, Led Zeppelin, Elton John, Blondie, and Garbage. She attended New York University's Tisch School of the Arts but dropped out to pursue a music career; not long afterward, in 2005, she was signed by Def Jam Records—then dropped a few months later. She began writing songs for pop artists, including Britney Spears and the Pussycat Dolls, while also performing in a burlesque show she created called Lady Gaga and the Starlight Revue. Singer-songwriter-producer Akon caught her act and signed her to his Interscope Records label, Kon Live Distribution.

She moved to Los Angeles and assembled a creative team, which she named Haus of Gaga, inspired by 1960s pop artist Andy Warhol's Factory, a studio where he and his anointed "superstar" fellow artists gathered to make paintings and films as a collective. Her 2008 debut single, "Just Dance," became a hit, propelling the full-length album *The Fame*. The second single, "Poker Face," hit even bigger. Gaga grew into a phenomenon so quickly that the

171

next year, she put out a deluxe reissue of *The Fame* called *The Fame Monster*; she was on such a tear that two of the bonus tracks, "Bad Romance" and "Telephone," were massive hits, the latter as a duet with Beyoncé.

Gaga's roll continued through 2011's *Born This Way*. The title track from the album served as her activism thesis statement, with the spoken refrain: "Don't be a drag, just be a queen." In that same song, the openly Christian and bisexual pop star also sings, "I'm beautiful in my way / 'Cause God makes no mistakes."

Her crazy looks became legendary, every fashion choice a deliberate one, each one telling a story and generating headlines. "My fashion is about the urban woman in the year 3000," she explained. "I think about obscure, weird things and try to create a world around them." In 2011, *Rolling Stone* named her the actual "Queen of Pop," based on record sales and social media statistics, propelled by her ability to make news and her dedication to her fans and her causes. She had created a new model for pop stardom in the social media era.

As other pop stars followed her lead, Gaga's own power was diluted for a stretch. Her 2013 record, *Artpop*, didn't dominate culture like the others had. She described it as "a celebration and a poetic musical journey" that explored the "reverse Warholian" world of modern fame. This seemed like a culmination of an elaborate performance art project: her entire career as a pop star, which she built based on the legacies of the Pop Star Goddesses who came before her, namely Madonna. Though *Artpop* didn't sell like her first three albums, it still generated the catchy, on-brand song "Applause."

And it signaled that it was time for a massive image switch. "I do keep transforming into a new shell of me," she explained in an interview with the *New York Times Magazine*. "So, sure, there is an acting component to what I do, or a showbiz component to what I do. But the word 'acting,' it's hard for me to talk about in that way, because 'acting' to me almost implies faking it." In 2014, she traded in her outlandish fashions for slightly more grounded, classically glamorous looks as she promoted her new venture: an album of jazz duets with crooner Tony Bennett, then in his late eighties, called *Cheek to Cheek*. It won a Grammy.

In 2016, yet another Gaga emerged, this time wearing a wide-brimmed pink hat and with a hippie-rocker vibe. With the look came her album full of guitar-tinged Americana, *Joanne*, featuring introspective lyrics about love gone wrong ("Perfect Illusion," "Million Reasons") and female friendship ("Hey Girl," "Grigio Girls" from the deluxe edition). It became her fourth album to hit number 1 in the United States. It also once again referenced her Christianity, as she sings in "Million Reasons": "I bow down to pray / I try to make the worse seem better / Lord, show me the way."

By 2017, she reached a major American pop star milestone, performing the halftime show at the Super Bowl. But she did it in her own Lady Gaga way, incorporating behind-the-scenes footage of her preparation for the event into a revealing documentary, *Gaga: Five Foot Two*, which also brought to light her battle with the chronic disease fibromyalgia.

The next year, she played off her image in a movie role destined for her: Ally, a pop star engaged in a tragic romance with a washed-up, alcoholic rocker in *A Star Is Born*. She stole the film opposite director Bradley Cooper, scoring an Oscar for the smash song "Shallow" and a nomination for her acting performance.

In October 2018, she spoke at an *Elle* magazine Women in Hollywood event, where she wore an oversized, beige, boxy Marc Jacobs suit. Once again, she manipulated the power behind the "What did she wear?" coverage. In her speech, she said she had been sexually assaulted at age nineteen by someone in the entertainment industry, but, she added, she was "still not brave enough to say his name." Then she explained her wardrobe choice for the evening: "I tried on dress after dress today getting ready for this event, one tight corset after another, one heel after another, a diamond, a feather, thousands of beaded fabrics and the most beautiful silks in the world," she said, but none of them felt right in light of her feelings.

This may seem like a surprising statement from a woman who has built her fame on entertaining the world, thanks in large part to what she has worn. But Gaga's goddess power is using her entertainer's artifice to funnel attention to issues she cares about.

## Gaga's Ancient Goddess Sister
# GUANYIN

Guanyin spreads compassion, urging us to let go of judgments about others. Instead, she hopes we will see the best in others, eschewing gossip for love. Guanyin exists in several forms in several Buddhist cultures; known as Guanyin in Chinese, she is Avalokitesvara in Sanskrit and Kannon or Kanzeon in Japanese. She hears all the cries of suffering in the world and is sometimes depicted as thousand-armed, holding all the tools she needs to attend to that suffering. She is sometimes male, sometimes female—a gender switch Gaga has also toyed with.

## Invoke Gaga for

Speaking out for causes you believe in
Getting attention
Feeling good about yourself the way you are
Pulling off outlandish looks

## How to channel Gaga's goddess energy

Make a concrete, step-by-step plan for supporting a cause you believe in.

Change your image to better suit what you'd like to project to the world. Don't be shy! Give yourself the ultimate makeover with crazy-colored hair, edgy makeup, a hat, statement shoes, or the item at the vintage store you're not sure you can pull off.

Find a way to "perform" live—a dance class, an open mic, whatever suits your interests. Do it for the exhilaration; don't worry about whether you're "good enough."

## JOURNAL RIFFS

What is your superpower? Gaga's is dressing and performing in a way that gets attention. Yours might be organizing groups, throwing parties, persuading people, or any number of other skills. How can you then use it to support a cause—raise funds, recruit volunteers, or draw public attention?

If you could tell the entire world one message, what would it be?

## power songs

"Marry the Night"
"Grigio Girls"
"Applause"
"Born This Way"
"Paparazzi"
"Telephone"
"Hey Girl"

"The Edge of Glory"
"Joanne"
"Million Reasons"
"Shallow"
"Always Remember Us This Way"
"Heal Me"

"I'll Never Love Again"
"John Wayne"
"Sinner's Prayer"
"Angel Down"

# LAURA JANE GRACE

## Goddess of Finding Your True Self

*At eight* years old, Laura Jane Grace first started keeping a journal when her teacher in Italy—Laura Jane was a U.S. Army brat—assigned her to do so while taking a trip to the Dachau concentration camp in Germany. "As an eight-year-old, trying to understand what fascism was, who the Nazis were, what the Holocaust was—it was hard to process," she later said. "Writing helped me with that."

Writing down her feelings would become critical to Laura Jane's life. She would develop into a rock star, the lead singer of the punk band Against Me!, under her given name and gender assigned at birth, Tom Gabel. As Tom, one of her signature songs, "The Ocean," spoke volumes: "If I could have chosen, I would have been born a woman / My mother once told me she would have named me Laura."

In 2012, Laura Jane came out as transgender in an interview with *Rolling Stone*. She published a memoir, *Tranny,* drawing on old tour journals. She learned, during her

transition, to let other things in her life evolve as well: for instance, playing in-the-works songs at shows, then continuing to work on them before they made it onto an official record. She and Against Me! put out an entire themed record about her experience, *Transgender Dysphoria Blues,* in 2014, a project that began with her telling her bandmates she wanted to tell the story of a fictional transgender person; eventually, she revealed that it was about herself.

Even during her transition, Laura Jane focused on the writing as much as any of the life changes she was encountering. She spoke about the song "Fuckmylife666," for instance, to *Time* magazine: "The feeling I wanted to convey with it was really hard to feel like I got right: what it's like to transition when you're married to someone who is the embodiment of femininity. 'Silicone chest and collagen lips'—not to pat myself on the back, but that's a really tricky couplet to fit into a lyric!"

Her transition became part of a larger trend in entertainment, as pop culture began to embrace trans representation—*Orange Is the New Black* actress Laverne Cox was on the cover of *Time* that same year. Of course, Laura Jane had not been thinking about that leading up to this major life decision.

Those journals of hers had gone from reading, "This journal belongs to Tom Gabel," to "This journal belongs to Laura Jane Grace." She didn't have to share them with the world, and she didn't have to share the details of her transition with the world. She didn't have to build her identity as a rock star on her transition. But she did, and she made a difference by doing so, which is what makes her a goddess. Once, she burned her birth certificate onstage in North Carolina to protest the state's law requiring people to use the restroom designated for the gender they were assigned at birth. She criticized an Arcade Fire video featuring cisgender actor Andrew Garfield as a trans woman. She starred in a documentary web series called *True Trans*, telling her own story and those of other genderqueer people. She spoke in interviews about the stress she felt as a woman: "All of a sudden you're like—and now I'm still a public figure and now I face the fear of, *Do I look fat in this dress?* I have to do a photo shoot and I'm worried about the way I look, and I feel like all those pressures sometimes, from a transition standpoint, are so unrealistic to navigate in a public eye."

Laura Jane Grace was born Thomas Gabel on November 8, 1980, at the U.S. Army School of the Americas at Fort Benning, Georgia, the child of U.S. Army Major Thomas Gabel and his wife, Bonnie (née Grace). By junior high, Laura Jane had gotten into punk rock, nihilism, and anarchism.

As an army brat, she grew up in several places, including Tennessee, Italy, and Ohio, before her parents divorced and she, her mother, and her brother settled in Naples, Florida. There, she got involved with a church youth group and formed her first band, the Black Shadows, with a few other kids from the program. They performed covers of Queen's "Bohemian Rhapsody" and John Lennon's "Imagine" in front of congregations and at talent shows. However, she writes in her memoir that at school she "didn't fit in with my classmates in my new high school, and none of them befriended me, which was fine because I didn't want to be their friend anyway."

Laura Jane got into Poison, Def Leppard, and Bon Jovi. But punk rock became her identity for good reason. Punk, she told NPR, "served as a form of armor, because when you're wearing a big leather jacket with spikes on it and you're charging out your hair with Knox gelatin, I mean, you're, like, arming yourself."

She cut herself and numbed herself with drugs and alcohol, which fit in with the punk rock scene, she said. "I actively sought out self-destructive things like deciding, *I am going to smoke cigarettes. This tastes terrible, it just made me throw up, but I'm going to keep going until I like these cigarettes.* Thinking in my head, *How can I get a hold of drugs? How can I find cocaine?* . . . And that's like [at] 13 years old, because I didn't know . . . I had no resources. I had no one to turn to, to talk about it."

In 1997, Laura Jane dropped out of high school at age seventeen to pursue music full-time, naming her project Against Me!. She would continue to perform with that as her band name—featuring a shuffling roster of other members—for the next twenty-plus years. After a first, brief, and private marriage ended, Laura Jane remarried in 2007 to visual artist Heather Hannoura, and the two had a daughter together, Evelyn, in 2009. Laura Jane later said that her feelings of gender dysphoria "started coming back really strong" when her wife was pregnant, though it would be a few more years before she acted on them. They divorced in 2013, a few years after Laura Jane had come out with Heather's support.

After several years on indie labels, Against Me! signed to Sire Records, a division of Warner Music Group, in 2005, sparking the traditional punk-scene cries of "sell-out." The band's 2007 album on the label, *New Wave,* indeed brought them to new heights of popularity. But Laura Jane's coming out as trans in 2012 changed public perception of the band once again. Laura Jane had, of course, been struggling her entire life with her gender dysphoria. "The cliché is that you're a woman trapped in a man's body, but it's not that simple. It's a feeling of detachment from your body and from yourself. And it's shitty, man. It's really fucking shitty."

Laura Jane moved from Florida to Chicago in 2012 and embraced the town, signing with Bloodshot Records for her first non–Against Me! release, 2018's *Bought to Rot,* by Laura Jane Grace & the Devouring Mothers.

Her work since her transition has often offered advice in hopes of steering subsequent generations of confused kids away from her mistakes. As she sings on Laura Jane Grace & the Devouring Mothers' "China Beach," "Learn to trust yourself / No one else matters / . . . And always welcome failure."

## Laura Jane's Ancient Goddess Sister

# BUTTERFLY MAIDEN

The Butterfly Maiden represents transformation, a clear theme in Laura Jane Grace's trajectory. The Maiden's change "brings great blessings," according to Doreen Virtue's *Goddess Guidance Oracle Cards*, just as Laura Jane has used her own transformation to help others struggling with similar issues. Laura Jane has also written and talked about her own anxieties as she has come out as a transgender woman. The Butterfly Maiden acknowledges the difficulties and blessings of great change. She assures us that endings are also beginnings. In her Hopi Native American spiritual tradition, she guides the transition from one season of the harvest to the next. She brings spring's refreshed energy and the opening of cocoons. She is the goddess of emerging into beauty and taking flight.

## Invoke Laura Jane for

Embracing your own true identity
Evolving
Welcoming all parts of the gender spectrum that
show up in your own personality

## How to channel Laura Jane's goddess energy

Read through your old journals, noticing patterns and insights you may
have missed at the time. (Try not to wince . . . too much.)

Share something you're working on before it's "finished" and "perfect."

Find a demonstration or protest to go to.

## JOURNAL RIFFS

Write about a political issue that upsets you—explore why things
are the way they are, why this issue upsets you, and what,
if anything, can be done about it.

If you're cisgender, what do you think your life would be like if you
were assigned another gender identity at birth? Are there parts of that
identity you'd like to explore in your current life?

Look at those old journals of yours (if you found some) and write a
response or update to some of your old entries.

## power songs

"China Beach"
"Apocalypse Now
    (& Later)"
"Reality Bites"
"I Hate Chicago"
"Manic Depression"
"New Wave"

"White People for
    Peace"
"Stop!"
"Piss and Vinegar"
"Americans Abroad"
"The Ocean"
"Fuckmylife666"

"Transgender
    Dysphoria Blues"
"True Trans Soul
    Rebel"
"The Apology Song"

# MARIAH CAREY

## Goddess of Earned Divadom

*Mariah Carey* stood in the gym, cleavage on full display in a low-cut top and unzipped jacket, accessorized by a diamond necklace, pearl choker, fishnet stockings, high-heel booties, and two twenty-pound hand weights. Mariah knew it was the perfect Mariah moment: she posted a short video clip of herself pumping iron to her Instagram. When asked about it in a 2017 interview with *Billboard*, she laughed. "That was a nonsense routine right there," she said. "Dressing up in the ensemble and doing that was just me having fun and being silly."

Mariah knows who she is in her third decade of fame: a true diva, except for one detail—she doesn't take herself too seriously. She's had her public failures—that odd 2001 appearance on *Total Request Live* that the media dubbed a "breakdown," that 2016 botched live TV performance on New Year's Eve in Times Square. But her

legacy remains secure, with the most number 1 chart debuts of all time and the remarkable feat of adding a new classic to the Christmas canon with "All I Want for Christmas Is You," which continues to dominate every holiday season. As of 2018, she ranked as the artist with the second-most number 1 hits (as opposed to just debuts) of all time, behind only the Beatles. Mariah's passionate fans launched a successful online campaign to get her previous bomb, the 2001 *Glitter* soundtrack, to chart in 2018.

She's got this diva thing *handled.*

Mariah Carey was born March 27, 1970, in Huntington, New York, to aeronautical engineer Alfred Roy Carey and voice coach Patricia Carey. Mariah suffered feelings of outsiderness because of her mixed race: her father's African American and Venezuelan heritage combined with her mother's Irish American lineage. "I always felt kind of different from everybody else in my neighborhoods," she said. "I was a different person ethnically. And sometimes, that can be a problem. If you look a certain way, everybody goes, 'white girl,' and I'd go, 'No, that's not what I am.'"

She loved music, particularly Billie Holiday, Al Green, Gladys Knight, and Aretha Franklin. She began taking voice lessons at four years old. At age eighteen, she attended the CBS Records party that changed her life, thanks to her friend and mentor, singer Brenda K. Starr. There Mariah met Columbia Records president Tommy Mottola, who would sign her within a few days and would eventually become her husband in 1993. Her self-titled debut album came out in 1990 and produced four of her number 1 hits, starting with "Vision of Love." The record also earned her a Best New Artist Grammy in 1991.

Mariah's five-octave vocal range became her signature, highlighted particularly on her debut record and the follow-ups, 1991's *Emotions* and 1993's *Music Box*. Though her melismatic singing style would become dominant over the next few generations of female pop singers, so would another of her stylistic choices. Her 1995 album, *Daydream*, began to mix in more hip-hop and R&B, relying less on her extraordinary upper-register vocals and more on collaborations: she sang with Boyz II Men on "One Sweet Day" and incorporated rap breaks from Ol' Dirty Bastard on the remix for the single "Fantasy"—a radio-friendly, genre-crossing trick that remains in vogue to this day. The clear heir to Whitney Houston, she recorded the duet "When You Believe" with Whitney in 1998, but also continued to mix hip-hop and rap into her music, distinguishing herself from her forebear.

Her trajectory hit a bump when she divorced Mottola, ended her contract with Columbia, and signed a $100 million, five-album recording contract with Virgin Records in April 2001. It seemed as if things were going great, but then came her semi-autobiographical movie *Glitter*. In the promotional run-up to the film during the summer of 2001, Mariah made her infamously loopy appearance on *Total Request Live*, during which she handed out ice cream to the audience and stripped down to a halter top and hotpants. She was hospitalized for exhaustion soon afterward. Meanwhile, the movie and soundtrack were such critical and sales disasters that Virgin paid her $28 million to end her recent contract, and she switched again to Island Records. Her subsequent 2002 release *Charmbracelet* struggled to connect with listeners.

Mariah didn't rebound musically and commercially until 2005's *The Emancipation of Mimi*. (By 2009, she also managed to erase the stench of *Glitter* with a critically praised acting performance in the film *Precious*.) But she began to rebuild her image as a true diva with an iconic performance on MTV's home-tour show *Cribs* in 2002, being filmed on her treadmill in heels and getting into a bathtub wrapped in a towel. When asked about her possible rivalry with then-rising star Jennifer Lopez in the 2000s, Mariah deadpanned, "I don't know her." This video clip, from a German talk show called *Taff,* would circulate widely online and become a favorite meme and battle cry for Mariah fans.

The rise of social media allowed her to further bolster her persona as she posted photos of herself bathing while wearing a diamond necklace, earrings, and bracelets or riding the New York City subway in a ballgown. Her children with second (and now ex-) husband Nick Cannon, Moroccan and Monroe, have their own hashtag: #dembabies. When she injured her arm in 2013, she kept it in a bedazzled sling. She appeared in 2013 on *The Tonight Show with Jimmy Fallon* with a folding fan, she explained, "in case I felt a bad angle coming." In 2016, she built an entire reality series around this persona, *Mariah's World*. Highlights included a scene with two assistants lacing her into complicated shoes and a flirtation with a much-younger backup dancer who would eventually become her boyfriend. But in 2018, she added another layer to her image when she revealed in a *People* magazine interview that she has bipolar disorder, a diagnosis that dates back to her public meltdown and hospitalization in 2001.

Mariah has proven that divadom needn't be humorless or self-unaware. In fact, she tells us, the best divas are funny, smart, complicated, and in control of their sometimes messy, always glamorous lives.

## Mariah's Ancient Goddess Sister
# APHRODITE

The Greeks' Aphrodite is among the most famous of all goddesses because she brings love, beauty, pleasure, and passion. Mariah deserves nothing less. Aphrodite is the daughter of the powerful Zeus and symbolizes female beauty; Mariah is not only physically beautiful, but also, more importantly, plays up and celebrates her feminine energy like a true bombshell. Aphrodite has developed strong, cultish followings throughout history and across the world, just as Mariah has built one of the strongest of the Pop Star Goddess fandoms. In one story, Aphrodite's husband Hephaestus, the Greek god of blacksmithing, lavished her with jewelry to show his appreciation for her beauty. In art, she is usually depicted as gorgeous and voluptuous, often commanding the attention of crowds around her. Mariah can surely relate.

## Invoke Mariah for

Embracing your complications
Bringing your inner diva out
Laughing at yourself
Enduring failure

## How to channel Mariah's goddess energy

Celebrate your "anniversary"—which is what Mariah prefers to call her birthday—with all the festiveness you desire.

Dress up to hit the gym.

Take a luxurious bubble bath. Diamonds optional.

## JOURNAL RIFFS

What would your ultimate diva moment be?

What's the funniest thing about yourself?

When was a time that you survived public humiliation by laughing at yourself / with yourself?

## power songs

"I Don't Wanna Cry"
"Heartbreaker"
"Touch My Body"
"GTFO"
"A No No"
"Giving Me Life"
"Always Be My Baby"

"Fantasy"
"The Roof"
"Emotions"
"Honey"
"Shake It Off"
"Someday"
"Sweetheart"

"Vision of Love"
"Migrate"
"Obsessed"
"I Know What You Want"
"Butterfly"

# MARY J. BLIGE

## Goddess of Rising Above

*Mary J. Blige* spent her preteen years in the housing projects of the Bronx in New York City, surrounded by abused women. Her father, a troubled Vietnam veteran, beat her mother during the years before he abandoned the family. Most of the women in Mary's building, she later said, also suffered multiple forms of harm at the hands of men. "I'd never seen a woman ever treated right other than my grandmother," she said. She'd go on to experience her own abusive relationships, including being molested by a family friend. That led, she later said, to her abusing herself—with drugs and alcohol.

All the while, though, shards of hope shone through to her, in the form of music. She found her own empowerment there, and she shared it with other women.

This hasn't stanched the personal difficulties in her life, even as her star has continued to rise over the past

twenty-plus years. As recently as 2017, Mary endured a public divorce battle that resulted in her having to pay her ex-husband and former manager, Kendu Isaacs, $30,000 per month in spousal support—and prompted the judge in the case to admonish her for living beyond her means. Still, she continues to share her talents—and her pain—through her art.

Mary was born on January 11, 1971, in the Bronx. Her father left the family when she was four. She and her mother and sister spent some time in Georgia after the split, then returned to a housing project in Yonkers, New York. There, Mary learned another early lesson, for better or worse: "Everything was about how you look," she later explained. "Although you didn't *have,* it was about how you looked."

Before Mary even hit her teenage years, she knew she wanted a career in music. She dropped out of high school and joined a band. She recorded herself singing Anita Baker's "Caught Up in the Rapture" in a karaoke booth at the Galleria mall in White Plains, New York, and sent it to record labels. Her tape made its way to Jeff Redd, a rep for Uptown Records. Soon Uptown had assigned Mary to producer Sean "Puff Daddy" Combs to be developed as a solo artist.

Her debut album, *What's the 411?,* was released in 1992. It got great reviews and was noted as a breakthrough for fusing hip-hop and R&B—that is, combining samples and beats traditionally used by rap artists with Mary's soulful vocals. Mary herself raps on the title track, while on "Intro Talk," she features a guest rap from then-newcomer Busta Rhymes. *And* she covers Rufus and Chaka Khan's funk classic "Sweet Thing." The track "Love No Limit," meanwhile, displays jazz influences. The album became a hit, peaking at number 6 on the *Billboard 200*; it ultimately went three times platinum. The record also set a theme for Mary's material overall, with three heartbreaking tracks: "I Don't Want to Do Anything," "My Love," and "Changes I've Been Going Through."

Mary would go on to be known as the "Queen of Hip-Hop Soul" over the course of twelve more studio albums, more than $75 million in record sales, and nine Grammy wins. She would build a respected acting career as well, earning an Oscar nomination in 2018 for her work in the film *Mudbound*. At that exact same time, however, she also found herself in the middle of the acrimonious divorce from her husband of twelve years, $6.5 million in debt to the IRS for back taxes, and even temporarily without a home as she tried to sell the New Jersey mansion she shared with her ex.

The breakup of her marriage echoed the (fictional) lyrics of her 1996 song "Not Gon' Cry," a kiss-off to a cheating spouse from the soundtrack to the movie *Waiting to Exhale*: "Eleven years out of my life / Besides the kids I have nothing to show / Wasted my years a fool of a wife." Her 2001 hit "No More Drama" gave her a catchphrase and a goal—but the goal was clearly more of an aspiration for her than an achievable end point. Her other huge hit of the same time, "Family Affair," perhaps more accurately stated her way of coping—not killing the drama, just flowing with it. "Come on baby just party with me / Let loose and set your body free / Leave your situations at the door."

Mary always pours the pain into her music. "The journey that got us here is one that every woman can relate to, a woman out there fighting for her marriage," she told *People* magazine when her 2017 album, *Strength of a Woman*, came out after her divorce. "When I first started writing [the album], I was fighting for my marriage. There were a lot of layers to me peeled back for this marriage. I really thought I did [find] the love of my life."

The album's title song, "Strength of a Woman," became the official anthem for the Women's National Basketball Association that year, a source of pride for Mary. She drew parallels between female athletes and female musicians: "As women, we have to fight to be taken seriously. We have to fight for people to understand that you stand there on that same level."

She found her own power, she said, in her faith in God—and in her own vulnerability through song. "The thing is, it's never been challenging," she said of sharing her deepest feelings and failings in her music. "It's a thing that I've always had to do."

That ability attracted new—and needed—artistic opportunities as she hit the low point of her divorce.

Director Dee Rees was preparing to make a film about racial strife on a Mississippi tenant farm after World War II, *Mudbound,* and wanted Blige to play the lead role of Florence, a plain, reserved woman with a well of unexpressed emotion. She imagined Blige's stage persona turned inside out: calm on the outside, simmering on the inside. "With Mary's music, if you've been to her concerts, it's literally like a therapy session for thousands of people," Rees said. "She's not just performing; she's living it. Every verse, she's reliving the heartbreak or she's reliving the joy, and you feel it."

Mary found herself grateful for the opportunity to grow. "As an artist you know when it's time to branch out into a whole new area when you become, in the eyes of your fans, [Michael] Jordan," she said of her music career. "I can do this asleep. Mary J. Blige, the singer, the Queen of Hip-Hop Soul—that's my game, I won." Just because she welcomed the challenge didn't mean it was easy to execute. "I didn't realize how vain I was until I started working on *Mudbound,*" she said. "Once I saw how my character, Florence, lived [in a shack on a farm in Mississippi], I thought, Wow, I'm really a vain person. When I went to the movie set to do the first day of fittings, I was Mary J. Blige: I had just done a tour and a show, so I was all, you know, I had wigs and weaves and all sorts of things going on, and Dee Rees was like, 'No! We want to see you. You can't have a perm, you're going to have minimal, minimal makeup.'"

Mary accepts and transforms her drama into art. Since she became a born-again Christian during her struggles with addiction, she has credited God for helping her transmute her pain in healthier ways. Whatever the source of her strength, she has helped countless fans enduring similar hardships, who found courage and power in her music.

By the time of *Strength of a Woman*, her thirteenth album, she understood her own abilities. "Some artists reject equating their personal lives with their artistic ones," a Pitchfork review began. "In the tradition of the most magnificent women in soul, Mary J. Blige has always invited it, freely discussing her travails and liberally exploring them within her songs, no matter how cutting." The album debuted at number 1 on *Billboard*'s R&B chart.

On her forty-eighth birthday in 2019, Mary posted a series of photos of herself in leopard-print bikinis, her long, golden waves shining in the sun; one photo was captioned, "LIVING MY BEST FUCKIN LIFE!"

When it comes to Mary, that doesn't mean she'll never have another problem. It just means when she does, she'll deal with it, set it to music, and move forward.

She says she has one remaining goal: "I want, at some point, to not have to work so hard. I want peace of mind and acceptance of self, totally." We'll always be cheering her on—and hoping for the same for ourselves.

## Mary's Ancient Goddess Sister
# DURGA

Durga is the "warrior goddess of protection" in Hinduism, as Sally Kempton says in her book *Awakening Shakti*. In Durga's creation myth, she saves the world after it is conquered by the egotistic, demon—male—warriors Shumbha and Nishumbha. She confronts them with her own power, as well as that of the magical lion she rides, and defeats them. Durga doesn't give her followers advice; she lends them her strength and expects them to put it to its best use in their own lives. In more modern terms, Durga resembles Wonder Woman. Durga's warrior spirit helps to fight addictions, transform personal challenges, or inspire spiritual awakening. She slays demons. She faces a challenge with courage. Or, in Mary's case, multiple challenges—with enduring courage and unshakeable faith that she'll always make it through.

## Invoke Mary for

Rising above your circumstances
Demanding better treatment from others
Overcoming addictive behaviors
Transforming pain into art

## How to channel Mary's goddess energy

Think of the most difficult issue in your life right now. Paint, draw, write, or choose another way of expressing your feelings about it through creativity.

Have a girls' night to blow off steam and find strength in other women.

Envision your dream career and map out a plan for getting it.

Leave behind any dead-end relationships in your life.

Dance out your troubles.

Work out to let go of stress.

## JOURNAL RIFFS

What is a new form of creative expression you'd like to explore more? Painting, drawing, sculpture, acting, writing, poetry, a musical instrument? What can you do to pursue it?

Write about the greatest achievement of your life. What's the "game" you "won," like Mary becoming the Queen of Hip-Hop Soul? What are you the queen of? How did you get there?

What is your "beauty regimen" that has nothing to do with products or treatments? What makes you glow from the inside?

## power songs

"Be Without You"
"Not Gon' Cry"
"Family Affair"
"Real Love"

"Enough Cryin"
"Good Woman Down"
"Baggage"
"MJB Da MVP"

"Ain't Really Love"
"Father in You"
"One"
"I'm Goin' Down"

# Goddess of Fierce Political Statements

*M.I.A. had* spent the last minute and forty-five seconds gyrating with golden pom-poms, dressed like a Roman cheerleader in a red-and-gold miniskirt and black thigh-high boots. *Cheerleader* did not compute in her standard M.O., so when it came time for her rap break in Madonna's "Give Me All Your Luvin'," she was ready to make a statement. She ended her part defiantly, though as scripted: "Imma say it once, yeah, I don't give a sh—" She didn't complete the swear word, as per U.S. broadcast guidelines. Eight years after Janet Jackson's career was destroyed in the same circumstances by a fraction-of-a-second shot of her bare breast and covered nipple, the risk surely didn't seem worth it.

M.I.A. didn't say "shit" during the 2012 Super Bowl halftime show. But she did flip the camera the middle finger just afterward. Statement made.

The National Football League sued her, asking for millions of dollars in damages and an apology. She and her lawyers responded by mocking that the league's "claimed reputation for wholesomeness" could be destroyed by

M.I.A.'s finger, what with the NFL's domestic abuse problems and the sport potentially causing life-altering brain trauma in many players. The suit was settled under undisclosed terms.

The goddess had appeared before a nation, in her element.

M.I.A., who goes by the name Maya, was born Mathangi Arulpragasam on July 18, 1975, in London, but her family moved to her father's native country, Sri Lanka, when Maya was just six months old. Her father, Arul Pragasam, became a separatist activist on behalf of his ethnic minority group, the Tamil, as a founding member of the Eelam Revolutionary Organisation of Students. His cause would become hers as well, and his life as an activist would infuse her work.

During the Sri Lankan Civil War, the family moved around several times within Sri Lanka, cut off from communication with Maya's father. She has described a life of poverty, with soldiers shooting at and destroying her grade school. When Maya was ten, her mother, Kala, moved with Maya and her two siblings to London as refugees. Kala worked as a seamstress to the British royal family. Maya likes to say that at the time, she knew only two English words: "Michael" and "Jackson."

Maya studied film at the prestigious Central Saint Martins in London, and as she segued into music, she did her own graphic design for album covers. She also used her music career to spotlight Tamil and other causes. Her

2004 mixtape with American DJ (and her sometime boyfriend) Diplo, *Piracy Funds Terrorism*, came out swinging by comparing illegal downloaders to suicide bombers. Her first studio album, *Arular*, named for her father and recorded in her London bedroom, dropped in 2005. She used tiger imagery in her promotional materials and often wore tiger-striped clothing, a reference to the Liberation of Tigers Tamil Eelam, a militant group fighting for a separatist Tamil state in Sri Lanka. As her fame grew, the media alternately labeled her a terrorist sympathizer or a naive pop star who didn't know what she was talking about.

But her 2007 album, named after her mother, *Kala*, earned her worldwide recognition. It sounded unlike the work of any other popular artist, with an international flavor: the single "Boyz" uses urumee drums, a trademark of Tamil music, but also incorporates soca music, while the lyrics reference Jamaican dance moves. The massive hit "Paper Planes," cowritten by Diplo, samples British punk group the Clash's "Straight to Hell," features gunshots and a cash register *ching* as rhythmic elements, and satirizes public perception of immigrants. "If you catch me at the border I got visas in my name," she sing-song-raps. The refrain, delivered like a nursery rhyme, goes: "Some some some I some I murder / Some I some I let go."

She performed at the 2009 Grammy Awards while nine months pregnant, wearing a skintight, mostly see-through black minidress. Labor contractions began as she rapped alongside Jay-Z, Kanye West, Lil Wayne, and T.I., whose song, "Swagga Like Us," sampled "Paper Planes." She said after, she believed that all the testosterone in the air had induced her labor.

Three days later, she gave birth to her son, Ikhyd. His father is her then-fiancé Benjamin Bronfman, a musician, an environmentalist, and the son of then–Warner Music Group CEO and Seagram's heir Edgar Bronfman Jr.

She would not, it seems, soften much with motherhood, with age, or with the end of the Sri Lankan conflict in 2009. As she reminded us in 2012 at the Super Bowl, she does not give a shit. In 2010, she tweeted the phone number of a *New York Times* writer who profiled her, noting contradictions such as M.I.A.'s championing of the poor while purchasing multiple houses for herself and eating truffle fries during the interview. In a 2016 interview with the *Evening Standard* she complained that Americans were paying too much attention to the Black Lives Matter movement, at the expense of other causes. She called out fellow Pop Star Goddess Beyoncé for exacerbating the problem by not speaking out about the plight of Syrians or violence against Muslims. In 2017, M.I.A. took issue with Diplo on Instagram for claiming he "discovered" her, accusing him of "distorting history." For her outspokenness and propensity for feuds, she's earned the nickname "the female Kanye."

She insists she isn't operating at 100 percent defiant at all times. "People think I walk around like I'm in a superhero movie, like I'm a villain in a trench coat stirring up trouble, I'm like the female version of the Joker," she said in a 2016 interview with Consequence of Sound. "And they don't realize that's not who I am." Later in the interview, she added, "The breadth and the width a human can stretch is vast. We don't have to live on this giant rock called Earth and limit ourselves to one way of thinking of who we are."

To wit, M.I.A. has shown that on occasion she knows how to let go and have fun, even while still making a statement. Her 2010 smash "Bad Girls" pays tribute to female sexual agency, combining her trademark sing-rap delivery with dancehall elements and syncopated beats. Its pure lyrical swagger evokes male rappers: "My chain hits my chest when I'm banging on the dashboard / My chain hits my chest when I'm banging on the radio." The video ups the ante, combining what could be stock American rap video images—speeding cars skidding out, gyrating female dancers—with a Middle Eastern desert setting full of crumbling buildings that appear to be war-ravaged, burning oil tankers, women in niqabs driving, and men in keffiyeh, the dancers dressed in flashy versions of traditional Middle Eastern clothing. It gives the middle finger to traditional Middle Eastern sexism *and* to Western anti-Muslim sentiment, dressed up in what sounds like nothing more than a fun pop song.

It's become the go-to anthem for female heroism on shows like *Orphan Black* and *The Mindy Project*. The women of *Saturday Night Live* did an epic send-up of the video in 2015, setting the music to scenes of the women doing bad-girl, middle-class American stuff like using the complimentary water cup at a fast-food restaurant for fountain lemonade, taking an elevator for just two floors, and leaving an unwanted container of ice cream on the bread shelf in the supermarket.

And by 2016 and beyond, M.I.A.'s politics didn't seem so extreme. Her song "Borders"—with lyrics that talk about police shootings, identities, and privilege, and a video featuring what could be a prototype for then–U.S. presidential candidate Donald Trump's wall at the Mexican border—could almost as easily have come from a high-minded American pop star, who would have been lauded for her bravery. Now M.I.A. sounded much more like the voice of reason; she'd seen it coming before the rest of us. "Well, I think I've been saying the same thing since 2005, but in 2016, we've become more divisive," she told Consequence of Sound. "We have all the governments getting super right-wing in Europe, and Trump wants to build walls, and all this stuff is just normal to everyone." But she also noted how music continued to bring people together: "You go to a festival, you listen to music from a DJ that's influenced by so many cultures and ideas, people's fashion, the way people dance. Culture progressed in a very mixed way, and then suddenly we have to separate and divide. And it's fear."

One sure antidote to such fear: M.I.A.'s music and attitude.

## M.I.A.'s Ancient Goddess Sister
# MATANGI

Maya's full name, Mathangi, comes from a Hindu goddess of music, Matangi. "She's basically a goddess of inner thoughts—the outward expression or the outward articulation of inner thoughts," Maya explained of her goddess namesake. "She was really interesting because she lived in the slums; she lived with the untouchables and represented them. So it was really cool to find a goddess that was not considered clean and pure, and was not on a pedestal." In fact, she explained to NPR, in a symbolic hand gesture called the Matangi mudra, the middle finger extends—so *that's* what she was doing in that Super Bowl performance.

It turns out to be true. The actual Matangi mudra shows the hands clasped and both middle fingers up, steepled together.

## Invoke M.I.A. for

Speaking out about political beliefs

Making a provocative statement

Not giving a shit

Defying authority

Keeping it real

Embracing your heritage

Infusing your work with activism

## How to channel M.I.A.'s goddess energy

Take in the art of other cultures for new inspirations.

Just walk down the street listening to "Bad Girls" in your earphones.

Swagger to your heart's content.

## JOURNAL RIFFS

What transgressions would you like to get away with in your version of the "Bad Girls" video?

What is the political belief you hold most dear? Why?
How can you work to express that in the world?

## power songs

"Go Off"

"Y.A.L.A."

"Borders"

"Bad Girls"

"Paper Planes"

"Boyz"

"Freedun"

"Bucky Done Gun"

"Temple"

"Double Bubble Trouble"

"Come Around"

"Exodus"

"Bamboo Banga"

"A.M.P."

"Galang"

"Matangi"

# MIRANDA LAMBERT

## Goddess of Unapologetic Spirit

*Miranda Lambert* arrived at a recording studio in July 2015 "ready to let off some steam," as songwriter Shane McAnally later described it to *Billboard*. News of Miranda's divorce from fellow country star Blake Shelton after four years of marriage had hit Twitter earlier that day. In "about five minutes," said McAnally, she and McAnally wrote her song "Vice." Its lyrics had a damn-the-torpedoes quality characteristic of Miranda: "Another bed I shouldn't crawl out of / . . . Said I wouldn't do it, but I did it again."

"I walked in with guns blazing," Miranda recalled. The album that included "Vice," *The Weight of These Wings,* resulted from a year's worth of such writing sessions. "I was like, 'Let's feel it all,'" she said. "I was ready to have the days where I can't even stand up and the days where I'm celebrating."

She had come a long way since growing up as an "east

Texas redneck girl," as she has described herself. Public life and romance had always stressed Miranda out; being country music's next Johnny and June or Tim and Faith came with a lot of pressure. But she understood it was a requirement of following her music dreams. A year into her marriage to Blake, she still had her own separate seven-hundred-acre property in Tishomingo, Oklahoma, that she'd bought before their 2011 wedding; she kept it and went there sometimes to wind down and enjoy being alone.

Meanwhile, she cozied up his place, where deer heads lined the walls, with her own touches—throw pillows, homemade peanut butter pie, and Yankee Candle Company cinnamon and pumpkin spice scented candles. She reported to *Good Housekeeping* that Blake had told her, "You really know how to make a house a home." When they were still married, she loved to sit on the porch with her husband while sipping a drink she invented that she called the "Mirandarita": Bacardi Light, Crystal Light Raspberry Lemonade, and Sprite Zero.

During her marriage to Shelton, Miranda often painted her life as a vision of suburban bliss in interviews. But she balanced that wifely image with badass lyrics ("Gunpowder & Lead" is about waiting, shotgun in hand, for an abusive boyfriend) and a fierce feminist streak; in 2011 she started a side musical project, Pistol Annies, with Ashley Monroe and Angaleena Presley. Post-divorce, her resolve on behalf of female power grew even stronger: her 2019 Roadside Bars & Pink Guitars tour featured only female acts. And she complained when her 2018 duet with Jason Aldean, "Drowns the Whiskey," hit number 1 on the *Billboard* Country Airplay chart. She pointed out to the *Washington Post* that she "had to sing with someone with a penis to get a number-one." Or, to put a "positive" spin on her attitude, as she said during the 2018 CMT Artists of the Year show, "Not a day will go by that I don't honor and lift up women in this industry."

Miranda Lambert was born November 10, 1983, in Longview, Texas. Growing up, she competed in regional country music talent shows, including Johnnie High's Country Music Revue in Arlington, Texas, the talent show that had helped the industry to discover LeAnn Rimes. Miranda launched her career by releasing her first, self-titled and self-released album in 2001 and appearing on the reality singing competition show *Nashville Star* in 2003. (She came in third place.) She signed with Epic Records that year. Her sweet, romantic 2004 single, "Me and Charlie Talking," found some success and helped to boost her 2005 album, *Kerosene,* to more than one million sales. Her 2007 follow-up record, *Crazy Ex-Girlfriend,* took her career to the next level.

Amid her rise to fame, she met Shelton in 2005 at CMT's 100 Greatest Duets concert. Shelton was married to first wife, Kaynette Williams, at the time he and Lambert were paired up to sing the 1981 David Frizzell and Shelly West song "You're the Reason God Made Oklahoma." Shelton filed for divorce from Williams a year later, after three years of marriage. He and Miranda went public with their relationship at the CMT Music Awards in 2007. They worked together on a record for the first time with Shelton's 2008 cover of Michael Bublé's "Home," with Miranda singing backup. They toured together in 2008 and cowrote several songs over the years, including Miranda's "Me and Your Cigarettes," "Love Song," and "Sin for a Sin" from her 2009 album, *Revolution.* He proposed in 2010 while they were strolling together around her Oklahoma property.

Gossip about their possible impending divorce began in 2013, though such rumors are standard for most famous married couples. And in the end, both Shelton's and Miranda's careers survived—and thrived—after their 2015 split. He became a household name as a permanent judge on *The Voice,* where he met Pop Star Goddess Gwen Stefani, whom he began dating soon after his divorce from Miranda. Meanwhile, Miranda wrote more than seventy songs post-divorce, with twenty-four ending up on her next album. She dated fellow musicians Anderson East and Evan Felker. Miranda switched publicity tactics thereafter, refusing to give interviews in advance of the 2016 release of *The Weight of These Wings.* The album became her first to debut at number 1. She bought a $3.4 million, four-hundred-acre farm property with three residences on it in Tennessee to replace her other place, which was in Shelton's home state of Oklahoma.

Miranda's brand, no longer dependent on her ex-husband's, blossomed into a clothing line called Idyllwind (a lifestyle brand for "boss ladies"), a Texas boutique called Pink Pistol, and the Red 55 Winery line. She married again in 2019, to New York City police officer Brendan McLoughlin. He hews closer to her Texas upbringing than he appears to: her father was a police officer who also ran a detective agency with her mother.

*The Weight of These Wings* proved to be her next-level moment. No less than *The New Yorker* said the album "defies Nashville wisdom—and is one of the year's best releases." Pitchfork noted it was a breakup record "refreshingly devoid of spite or anger."

In fact, Miranda's superpower is running the gamut of emotions. As she told a crowd during a 2018 concert: "I make it my mission every single time I step on the stage that no matter what, no matter where I am, I want to make you feel everything you could possibly feel. I want you to feel sad, mad, happy, and nostalgic and really pissed sometimes."

That last one, she added, is her favorite.

## Miranda's Ancient Goddess Sister
# PELE

Pele denotes the "divine passion" that comes from being honest and true to your own desires, according to Doreen Virtue's *Goddess Guidance Oracle Cards*—a perfect match with Miranda's standard M.O. in her love life and career. Both Pele and Miranda feel every bit of their own inner workings, which aren't so easy for all of us to access. These goddesses throw off the constraints of trying to please others. From pursuing her music career dreams to going after the love she wants, no matter the cost, Miranda stays true to a life philosophy that she once posted on Instagram: "I do this thing called whatever I want." Of course, this can cause an eruption: Pele is the Hawaiian goddess of volcanoes, and her destructive side has inspired fear and misunderstanding. Eruptions come as a necessary part of nature's cycles, even if they can sometimes be dangerous. The destruction can, metaphorically speaking, make way for the new.

## Invoke Miranda for

Expressing yourself without holding back

Letting off steam

Indulging your vices, at least a little

Getting in touch with your feelings

Following your dreams

## How to channel Miranda's goddess energy

Arrange for some quality alone time.

Put together a low-budget day of indulgence: peanut butter pie, Yankee Candles, and a Mirandarita will do just fine.

## JOURNAL RIFFS

Which women in your life could you help to support, whether it's through mentorship, joint projects, or friendship?

Miranda didn't mind calling herself a "crazy ex-girlfriend," even making it the title of her album. What's an "insult" you could embrace as your own?

## power songs

"Vice"

"Gunpowder & Lead"

"Crazy Ex-Girlfriend"

"Guilty in Here"

"Fine Tune"

"Fastest Girl in Town"

"Baggage Claim"

"Look at Miss Ohio"

"Nobody's Fool"

"Little Red Wagon"

"White Liar"

"Ugly Lights"

"Highway Vagabond"

"Well-Rested"

"Somethin' Bad"

"Getaway Driver"

# MISSY ELLIOTT

## Goddess of Powerful Weirdness

*A woman* dances to a sample of Ann Peebles's funk groove "I Can't Stand the Rain" in a metal-paneled cell, wearing what looks like a sparkly cycling helmet with built-in sunglasses and a luxe, black, shiny garbage bag ballooning around her. She is rapping to the camera at weird angles, unconcerned with being flattered by the shot, often distorted by a fish-eye lens: "I feel the wind, five six seven, eight nine ten / Begin, I sit on Hill's like Lauryn / Until the rain starts, comin' down, pourin' chill."

This might be what the future looks like, and sounds like. It is not what 1997 looked like, or sounded like, at least not until Missy "Misdemeanor" Elliott's video for "The Rain (Supa Dupa Fly)." Twenty-plus years later, Afrofuturism would go more mainstream, with the worldwide success of *Black Panther,* Jay-Z's "Family Feud" video, and

Janelle Monáe's entire body of work. Missy was ahead of even the future of the future.

Missy was not trying to be cute or sexy. She was selling her skill, vibe, and vision, nothing else, clearly meant to compete with the big boys of rap. "Elliott used her body, costumes, lyrical genius and sense of humor to craft a niche that remains her own to this day," Cameron Cook wrote on the music website Noisey in 2017. "Instead of using her sexuality to create a fantasy, she used it to create a mystery."

Her debut album, *Supa Dupa Fly*, prompted a rare honor for a new artist: a fawning, thinky profile in *The New Yorker*. Hilton Als wrote: "Generally, the New Negro—who is 'new' every decade or so—is female, a woman who considers her marginal status a form of freedom and a challenge: she takes the little she has been given and transforms it into something complex, outrageous, and, ultimately, fashionable." He continued, "Missy (Misdemeanor) Elliott, the twenty-five-year-old hip-hop performer who is energetically redefining the boundaries of rap music, is a singer, a songwriter, an arranger, a producer, and a talent scout. . . . She is the biggest and blackest female rap star that Middle America has ever seen. She is the latest incarnation of the New Negro."

Melissa Arnette Elliott was born July 1, 1971, in Portsmouth, Virginia. In the early 1990s, she formed an R&B girl group with three friends called Fayze, then renamed Sista; she recruited a neighborhood friend, Timothy Mosley, to produce them. The group signed with a label and recorded an album, but it was never released. After they disbanded, Missy continued to write with Mosley, now known as Timbaland. The two began to get traction in the mid-1990s, placing some songs on Aaliyah's album *One in a Million*, and writing for 702 and SWV. Their writing led to Missy being featured as a rapper on songs by Raven-Symoné (just seven and fresh off her run as the precocious Olivia on *The Cosby Show*), New Edition, MC Lyte, Lil' Kim, and others.

"The Rain (Supa Dupa Fly)" came as the lead single on Missy's 1997 debut album, *Supa Dupa Fly*. Produced by Timbaland and recorded in just a week, the album featured an innovative mix of hip-hop, dance, electronica, and R&B that was a hit with critics and listeners—it debuted at number 3 on the *Billboard* charts and went platinum in the United States. "The radio is stuck right now," Missy told MTV News. "Everything sound the same. As far as video-wise everything look the same. So we coming in to change the whole thing." The trash-bag suit from the video became iconic—so much so that Missy dressed up as her 1997 self in a similar getup for Halloween in 2018, and fellow Pop Star Goddess Solange wore a puffer-jacket homage to the look for the Met Gala in 2017.

Writing about *Supa Dupa Fly* in retrospect, *The New Yorker*'s Doreen St. Félix said, "The album is a treatise on that ineffable feeling of 'flyness.' (The title track itself is a play on the 1972 blaxploitation film *Super Fly*.) It is a testament to black ownership of black tradition. With her fantastical costumes, her oily ability to slip from singing to rapping to elliptical riffing, Elliott was a master inheritor of the black-American art of rule-breaking." Missy has continued to collaborate with Timbaland, for twenty years and counting, and their work together has elevated him to one of the most in-demand and distinctive producers in the industry.

This high-art-level respect for her work allowed Missy to escape many of the typical trappings of celebrity. She hasn't had high-profile relationships, scandals, or feuds. She doesn't dress in high fashion, favoring (high-end) baseball caps and sweat suits for her stage shows. She displays her fun-loving personality at times during media appearances, but her reputation rests upon her accolades: she was the first female rapper to receive an honorary doctorate from the prestigious Berklee College of Music and to be inducted into the Songwriters Hall of Fame.

*Essence,* when honoring Missy with its Black Women in Music award, called her "a consummate visionary whose creativity knows no limits" and who "has continuously pushed the boundaries in her work to shift the culture for the better across multiple industries including music, dance, fashion, film, television and art."

It follows that Missy counts Beyoncé, Solange, and Katy Perry among her famous fans. When Pop Star Goddesses look for someone to worship, they find Missy Elliott—the best of the best.

## Missy's Ancient Goddess Sister
# KALI

Many descriptions of Hindu goddess Kali reduce her to her doom-and-gloom aspects: she's depicted wearing a hula skirt of severed arms or a garland of skulls. But she is, in fact, the goddess of revolution. Kali is demonized in some quarters for good reason—she is a threat to the patriarchy. Another of her forms, Bhairavi, "erupts with the boundary-busting force of a volcano or massive forest fire," as Sally Kempton writes in *Awakening to Kali: The Goddess of Radical Transformation*, which sounds a lot like Missy's instant and profound effect on pop music. She burns everything down until we get to the source of true creativity, necessity being the mother of invention.

## Invoke Missy for

Embracing your most unique qualities
Manifesting your vision of the future
Exploring new creative paths

## How to channel Missy's goddess energy

Wear the most outrageous outfit you can come up with.
Put on some music and dance in the weirdest way possible.
Burn a candle, incense, or palo santo to symbolize the fire of creativity.

## JOURNAL RIFFS

What's the weirdest thing about you? How can you turn
that into a superpower?

What do you imagine the future will look like? What will
music sound like then?

## power songs

"Get Ur Freak On"
"Work It"
"Lose Control"
"I'm Better"

"The Rain (Supa Dupa
Fly)"
"One Minute Man"
"Gossip Folks"
"I'm Really Hot"

"WTF (Where They
From)"
"This Is Me"
"Hot Boyz"

# NICKI MINAJ

## Goddess of Beating Guys at Their Own Game

*Nicki Minaj* had done good work in the career that led up to her 2014 hit "Anaconda." Her trap masterpiece, "Beez in the Trap," for instance, or her flawless pop song, "Super Bass." But "Anaconda" did something else altogether: out of context, it could be dismissed as her rapping over a mega-hit from the past, Sir Mix-a-Lot's indestructible 1992 ode to big asses, "Baby Got Back."

But listen closer, and you hear Nicki at her greatest. She turns the tables on Mr. Mix-a-Lot, and then some. She names herself the object of his objectifying lyrics, then switches to subject mode, telling her own stories in her verses, explaining with a novelist's detail how she used her own ass to gain what she wanted from various men. Michael's verse wins, no doubt: "This dude named Michael used to ride motorcycles / Dick bigger than a tower,

I ain't talking 'bout Eiffel's." Incidentally, Michael is also the young man who "toss my salad like his name Romaine." *And* he bought her Balmain.

In 2016, Nicki became the bestselling female rapper of all time, no doubt in part because of "Anaconda."

Onika Tanya Maraj was born on December 8, 1982, in Trinidad and Tobago; she immigrated with her family to Queens in New York City when she was five. Her father, a drug addict, once tried to set the family home on fire in an attempt to kill her mother. As a young girl, the future rap star would create alternate personae to escape the reality of her life, and she dreamed of becoming an actress. She attended New York's famous Fiorello H. LaGuardia High School of Music & Art and Performing Arts, hoping to become successful enough to help her mother. "I've always had this female-empowerment thing in the back of my mind," she said in an interview with *Details,* "because I wanted my mother to be stronger, and she couldn't be. I thought, 'If I'm successful, I can change her life.'"

Nicki grew up admiring rapper Foxy Brown, one of the few major female rappers at the time: "I was really interested in her mind and her aura," Nicki said. And she idolized Jay-Z, on whom she has modeled her own career: "Me and my friends in high school, we were reciting all of the Jay lyrics," she said. (Google "Nicki Minaj slowed down" and you'll find out how closely connected the two are. At a fraction of her normal speed, Nicki's flow sounds eerily like Jay's.)

After performing in a group called the Hood$tars, Nicki put out three solo mixtapes between 2007 and 2009, and was then signed to rapper Lil Wayne's label, Young Money Entertainment. With the release of her 2010 debut album, *Pink Friday*, came a heightened image, full of exaggerated wigs, extreme pastel makeup, and Halloween-level costumes. She wore pink wigs, white wigs, green wigs, multi-colored wigs. Bubblegum-pink lipstick became one of the few consistent features of her looks.

Her breakout moment came when she contributed a verse to the 2010 rap powerhouse collaboration "Monster," a Kanye West track featuring Jay-Z, Rick Ross, and Nicki. An early line warns: "You could be the king, but watch the queen conquer." In one verse, she cycles through at least three characters with distinct flows and voices. Then she concludes: "Pink wig, thick ass, give 'em whiplash / I think big, get cash, make 'em blink fast / Now look at what you just saw, this is what you live for." West later claimed he'd thought about taking Nicki off the record because she was so good—though, in true Kanye fashion, he managed to self-aggrandize even while paying her the ultimate compliment: "It was like that moment when I thought about taking Nicki's verse off of 'Monster' because I knew people would say that was the best verse on the best hip-hop album of all time, or arguably top ten albums of all time," he said, with a late pivot toward modesty.

Nicki's skill has led to her being recognized as one of the best rappers ever, and she's the only woman to be featured on *Forbes*'s Hip-Hop Cash Kings annual list, starting in 2011. (Note the gender exclusion inherent in its name. In fact, Nicki didn't make the 2018 list, which was back to an all-male lineup.) But she has also achieved a rare level of crossover success into mainstream pop, starting with her 2012 album, *Pink Friday: Roman Reloaded,* thanks to dance-infused hits such as "Starships," on which she also sings. As evidence of her pop appeal, she opened for Britney Spears's 2011 Femme Fatale Tour.

Nicki has achieved mainstream pop culture ubiquity with appearances in movies like 2014's *The Other Woman* or as an animated character's voice in 2012's *Ice Age: Continental Drift.* Her focus on female empowerment has produced collaborations with the highest-level female pop stars, including fellow Pop Star Goddesses Beyoncé and Ariana Grande. Nicki's 2014 duet with Beyoncé, "Feeling Myself," celebrates female sexual agency like few pop hits before it: "'Cause I'm feelin' myself, jack off / He be thinking about me when he whacks off / Whacks on? Wax off."

But Nicki's appeal goes beyond explicit lyrics. Her 2010 collaboration with Drake, "Moment 4 Life," hits a purely inspirational note, drawn from her triumph over her difficult upbringing: "I fly with the stars in the skies / I am no longer trying to survive / I believe that life is a prize."

She's often used her platform to inspire her fans, encouraging them to stay in school and take advantage of their studies. She has paid off several fans' student loans and school bills. She preaches a take-control attitude to the girls who look up to her: "I always feel it's important for me to show females that they can be in charge of their own situation," she said. "I came into the game creating my own brand."

She even has some specific thoughts on salary negotiations: ask around and find out what your peers are making, even if it seems impolite. "I know it's taboo to discuss it at work," she told *Cosmopolitan*. "But you need to know what people around you are making. Otherwise, you're not going to know what you're worth. You have to ask questions. 'What is this person getting?' Do your research. I've always been pretty competitive in terms of my pay."

How else could she become not only the bestselling female rapper, but also a Hip-Hop Cash Queen?

Nicki, however, has a shadow side as a goddess. The internet has debated her feminist credentials, and for good reason. Despite her talk of female empowerment, she has feuded with a number of other female stars, including Cardi B, Remy Ma, and Mariah Carey. She doesn't care for competition from other women. "Every two years I get told about some new female rapper," she said. "To me, it's silly to compare me to women because there's no woman that can put up the stats that I've generated."

Nicki also lashed out at culture writer Wanna Thompson, who posted on Twitter: "You know how dope it would be if Nicki put out mature content? No silly shit. Just reflecting on past relationships, being a boss, hardships, etc. She's touching 40 soon, a new direction is needed." Nicki excoriated Thompson via direct message, which Thompson screenshot and posted. It wasn't pretty: "Eat a dick you hating ass hoe," Nicki wrote. "Just say u jealous. I'm rich, famous intelligent, pretty . . ." Nicki's fans followed her lead, harassing Thompson and sending her death threats.

This defensiveness may come from Nicki's drive to be recognized as not just a great female rapper, but a great rapper. And she has achieved this, according to many of her peers. "She made her own way and there's a gang of people, not only women, following her path," Lil Wayne said in a 2018 interview.

As of about 2014, Nicki also began to transform her look, relying less on visual gimmicks to distinguish herself. She has transitioned from extreme wigs and costumes to more natural hair and makeup with a wardrobe full of sleek, high-end fashion. For the 2014 MTV Movie Awards, she wore a long, black Alexander McQueen gown. She announced the release of her fourth album, *Queen*, from the red carpet at the fashion world's prestigious Met Gala in 2018. She continues to show off her stomach or cleavage in revealing dresses and crop tops, but she seems to have settled into being herself, rather than a cartoon character.

But no matter what look she chooses next, her goddess powers remain: she can play with the big boys and beat them every time.

## Nicki's Ancient Goddess Sister
# SARASWATI

Saraswati rules the realms of language, sound, and creativity; her name means "the flowing one." Knowledge and learning are paramount to the Hindu goddess, just as they are to Nicki. Saraswati knows how to use communication to her advantage, which can be through great poetry or through lies and deliberate disinformation. This is Nicki at her best and worst: making a place for women at the top of the rap game with her incredible skill and tearing down those who get in her way. Just as men have been doing for time eternal.

## *Invoke Nicki for*

Telling your own story

Asking for what you want in bed, in relationships, and in business

Being the best in your game

## *How to channel Nicki's goddess energy*

Figure out what you want in your career, then figure
out what training you need to get there. Sign up.

Find a signature look and commit to it.

Enjoy some solo time with a vibrator.

## JOURNAL RIFFS

What's your favorite curse word? Write about why.

Write about your greatest triumph.

List all the expectations you feel are placed on you by different people
and roles in your life. Which ones can you now start working to drop?

Write a rap verse introducing yourself to the world.

## power songs

"Monster"
"Turn Me On"
"Bang Bang"
"Beez in the Trap"
"Pound the Alarm"
"Super Bass"

"Feeling Myself"
"Anaconda"
"Starships"
"The Boys"
"Moment 4 Life"
"Bottoms Up"

"Side to Side"
"Barbie Dreams"
"Blazin'"
"Truffle Butter"

# PINK

## Goddess of Strength Through Motherhood

*Alecia Moore* was driving her six-year-old daughter, Willow, to school when Willow said, "Mama? . . . I'm the ugliest girl I know. . . . I look like a boy with long hair."

Alecia—a.k.a. the tomboyish pop superstar Pink—churns out rousing empowerment anthems regularly. And still, this is what her own daughter believed? Pink thought to herself, as she later said, "Oh my God, you're six. Why? Where is this coming from? Who said this? Can I kick a six-year-old's ass?"

Instead of saying any of that to her daughter, Pink went home and made a PowerPoint presentation featuring androgynous rock stars like David Bowie, Freddie Mercury, Annie Lennox, Prince, Janis Joplin, George Michael, and Elton John. "When people make fun of me, that's what they use," she told Willow. "They say I look like a boy or I'm too masculine or I have too many opinions. My body is too strong." Pink went on to explain

that she had not changed the way she looked to fit others' expectations, and yet she continued to sell out arenas all over the world.

When Pink told this story while accepting the MTV Video Vanguard Award in 2017, she concluded, addressing her daughter, "So, baby girl, we don't change. We take the gravel and the shell and we make a pearl. And we help other people to change so they can see more kinds of beauty."

This message has remained consistent throughout the powerhouse singer's twenty-year career. Her videos and performances always surprise and exceed expectations, and they always have a message—often one of empowerment for those who feel like outsiders. Her 2003 video for "Trouble" featured the singer kicking cowboys' asses to save abused horses. Her 2001 song "Don't Let Me Get Me" chronicled her own insecurities: "Tired of being compared to damn Britney Spears / She's so pretty / That just ain't me." Pink's 2008 song "So What" and its accompanying video have her celebrating her independence during a separation from husband Carey Hart: "I guess I just lost my husband / I don't know where he went / . . . I'm not gonna pay his rent."

Alecia Beth Moore was born on September 8, 1979, in Doylestown, Pennsylvania. She was performing in Philadelphia clubs by age fourteen. She joined a group called Choice, which was signed by LaFace Records. The label never released the group's record, though their single, "Key to My Heart," was included on the soundtrack to the

1996 Shaquille O'Neal comedy *Kazaam*. Label head L.A. Reid told Pink he'd sign her as a solo act, but Choice was done. The group parted ways in 1998.

Pink soon began recording a solo album, *Can't Take Me Home*, which launched with the 2000 single "There You Go," an R&B-inflected kiss-off to a pathetic boyfriend. ("Please don't come around talking 'bout how you changed / How you said goodbye to what's-her-name / All it sounds like to me is new game.") She cowrote that track and several others. It marked the first of a string of hits from the album, which also included "Most Girls" and "You Make Me Sick." With her short, spiky, hot pink hair, smoky eye makeup, and tough-girl patched jeans, she represented a clear alternative to the Britneys and Christinas of the day. Pink would go on to refine her punk-inspired style throughout her career, wearing different hairstyles, from rockabilly blond curls to a black asymmetrical crop.

She was, however, often lumped in with the poppier young women, to the point where she was rumored to have a feud with fellow Pop Star Goddess Christina Aguilera. Christina clarified years later that she felt rebuffed when Pink refused to kiss her during a game of Spin the Bottle. Pink said her memory was that Christina almost punched her once at a club. In any case, "I'm an alpha, and she's an alpha," Pink said, by way of explanation, in a 2017 interview. Pop Star Goddesshood at its finest.

As Pink's career progressed, so did her personal life:

at the 2001 Summer X Games in Philadelphia, she met motocross star Carey Hart, whom she began dating. She married him, separated from him, reunited with him, and wrote a lot of songs about their tumultuous relationship. In 2008, she released the song "So What" about their breakup, and a video featuring him playing himself—they patched things up while working on it together. They had Willow in June 2011 and son Jameson in December 2016. Pink wore her parenting proudly. She shared with *Cosmopolitan* the advice she was passing on to her daughter: "There's no such thing as success without failure." "It's very boring to be normal." "We don't say mean things and we don't say things we don't mean."

Pink told the magazine her daughter had asked her, "How many boys can I have at once?" Pink's answer: "Probably none of them because they won't deserve you."

Pink has even managed to make her demanding career a parenting asset, taking her kids on tour so "they get to see their mom be the boss," she told *Redbook*. She added, with a hint of sarcasm, "We've been on the tour bus for three days and I haven't slept, so that's great. I know this is going to be hard, but we'll make amazing memories."

Pink has never shied away from talking politics, going back to her pointed George W. Bush criticism in the 2006 song "Dear Mr. President." She's also counted among the most vocal pop star critics of President Donald Trump, whom she called "rock bottom." She tweeted a heartfelt plea to him in October 2017: "I've seen people change and turn their lives around. There's still hope for you @POTUS. It's what the world needs."

In fact, Twitter has served Pink's empowering messages well, allowing her to demonstrate, for instance, how to respond to a troll who mocked her by calling her "old": "You must be from LA. Well, there are a few people left in the world that choose to age naturally. I've earned every fucking minute of my 38 years." She continued: "I am of the mindset that it's a blessing to grow old. That if your face has lines around your eyes and mouth it means you've laughed a lot."

Such frank talk has proven Pink's greatest strength. She understands the limitations of aging in her line of work: "Statistically you can't be a pop star if you're over 35," she told *Financial Times* when she was thirty-eight, with a brand-new album out—*Beautiful Trauma*, her seventh.

She spoke in a 2017 interview with the *Guardian* about how hard long-term relationships are. "There are moments where I look at [Hart] and he is the most thoughtful, logical, constant . . . he's like a rock," she said. "He's a good man. He's a good dad. He's just the kind of dad I thought he'd be and then some. And then I'll look at him and go: I've never liked you. There's nothing I like about you. We have nothing in common. I don't like any of the shit you like. I don't ever wanna see you again. Then two weeks later I'm like, things are going so good, you guys. Then you'll go through times when you haven't had sex in a year. Is this bed death? Is this the end of it? Do I want him? Does he want me? Monogamy is work! But you do the work and it's good again."

More than anything, Pink knows her own feelings and is willing to share them all—and tries to teach her kids to do the same. "Willow won't cry ever, and it annoys me to no end," she told *Redbook*. "One day I had a sit-in at her school because I knew she was upset and she wouldn't talk to me. I sat down on the pavement and I was like, 'I'm not moving until you tell me about your feelings, because this is going to be a lifelong conversation for you and me and you have to learn to let me in.' Without batting an eye, she goes, 'I promise to tell you more about my feelings if you promise to tell me less about yours.'" Pink continued, "In my head I was like, *Holy s—t!* But I said, 'Not going to happen. People pay me for my feelings.'"

And we'll keep paying—a lot.

PINK

## Pink's Ancient Goddess Sister
# DAMARA

Celtic fertility goddess Damara helps to guide children through life, which is a skill Pink also has. Pink loves sharing what she's learned about motherhood, including her fears and her struggles, which in turn helps the millions of other moms reading or hearing her words. She reveals the difficult truths about being a wife, a parent, and a child, making her a kind of tough-love mother figure to us all. Damara, similarly, helps all households to function smoothly and wisely. Damara knows children's joy is infectious and inspiring to us all. She encourages us to spend time with children (our own or someone else's) and to communicate clearly and honestly with them. She also helps us tend to our own inner children.

## Invoke Pink for

Helping children work through insecurities

Embracing whatever gender expressions speak to you

Expressing your feelings and opinions

## How to channel Pink's goddess energy

Build up your muscles so you feel strong, physically and mentally.

Volunteer for an organization that helps children, animals,
or any other group you feel passionately about.

Cut your hair short or dye it a crazy color.

Take your kids—or someone else's kids—to work to teach them
about what you do and serve as a role model.

## JOURNAL RIFFS

Write a letter to our current president. Pour your heart out.

List the best things about being whatever age you are.

What advice would you give to a five-year-old? A ten-year-old?
A twenty-year-old?

## power songs

"Beautiful Trauma"

"So What"

"Please Don't
Leave Me"

"Who Knew"

"Leave Me Alone (I'm
Lonely)"

"U + Ur Hand"

"Conversations with
My 13-Year-Old
Self"

"Respect"

"Raise Your Glass"

"Stupid Girls"

"Blow Me (One Last
Kiss)"

"The Truth About
Love"

"Trouble"

"Dear Mr. President"

# QUEEN LATIFAH

## Goddess of Declaring Yourself Queen

*Queen Latifah* was just beginning a promising career as the rarest of the rare: a female rapper. But the fragility of such a situation didn't cause her to water her message down. The 1989 video for "Ladies First," from her debut album, *All Hail the Queen*, features portraits of black heroines such as Harriet Tubman and Angela Davis as well as scenes of violent clashes between black South Africans and white authorities under apartheid, interspersing them with more traditional video images of Latifah and collaborator Monie Love rapping, flanked by dancers.

A few years later, Latifah employed this tactic for another empowerment anthem, wrapping her political message in the trappings of hip-hop fun, using musical tricks to lull listeners into staying with her. During the first twenty-three seconds of Latifah's 1993 hit "U.N.I.T.Y.", a few measures of laid-back saxophone riff and a soft, tuneful vocal spelling out "U-N-I-T-Y" give way to Latifah spitting, "Who you callin' a bitch?"

Latifah has always led with the causes that mean the most to her—equality for women and people of color. And while some other rappers among the Pop Star Goddesses have given in to their competitive side, Latifah has reached out to help other female stars time and again throughout her thirty-year career. "We can't keep this thing going with one person," she said of women in hip-hop. "We need a bunch of us."

Her work made that possible. Her talent forced the hip-hop establishment to accept her, but her success wasn't the only reason more women could enter the genre after her. Women found more acceptance in the hip-hop world because Latifah didn't try to be one of the guys. She made it clear from the start: she was a woman, and she would not tolerate disrespect for herself *or* any other women.

Queen Latifah was born Dana Elaine Owens on March 18, 1970, in Newark, New Jersey. She started her music career beatboxing for the hip-hop group Ladies Fresh and performing with the collective Flavor Unit. She later explained her interest in the form: "I was attracted to the sound and the content and the freedom of rap. To me, it's like a free art form. It flows—it's smooth. It can be anything you want it to be—harsh, bitter, funny, you name it."

A recording of Latifah's song "Princess of the Posse" made its way to hip-hop legend Fab 5 Freddy, who was hosting *Yo! MTV Raps* at the time. From there, it got the attention of hip-hop label Tommy Boy Music, which signed her and released her first single, "Wrath of My

Madness," in 1989. It appeared on *All Hail the Queen,* along with "Ladies First."

"Ladies First" became one of her signature songs. The lyrics laid out her mission: "Some think that we can't flow / Stereotypes, they got to go / I'mma mess around and flip the scene into reverse." But she didn't rely on her femaleness to distinguish her style; she fused reggae and jazz with hip-hop, could both sing and rap, and highlighted her African heritage through her stage name and her style of dress. "Being Afrocentric and proud of my heritage, that's something I grew up with," she said. "My mother always taught me that."

The record eventually sold more than one million copies. With her newfound wealth, Latifah began to invest, first in a deli and video store on the ground floor of her apartment building. Just a few years later, she cofounded her own company, Flavor Unit Entertainment, in Jersey City, New Jersey, a business offshoot of the Flavor Unit collective in which she had started out. It would go on to manage and produce several rap artists, including Naughty By Nature and OutKast, and to produce television and films.

Despite the imagery of her videos and her lyrics' clear call for gender equality, she managed to convince people her music was apolitical. "What sexism?" she said in a 1991 *Baltimore Sun* interview. "That's a misconception propagated by the media. I didn't have one door slammed in my face because I was a woman." But in the same interview, she also excoriated male rappers' lyrics about women: "As far as women being referred to as 'bitches' and 'whores,' that's crap. I'm sick of hearing that. They may say they're talking only about certain women, but I don't buy that. They don't stop to think about the women they're offending. For many of the rappers, it's a state of mind, something they grew up with. These guys have that negative streak in them regarding women. That's why they say those nasty, vicious things."

She said she avoided too much political content in her own songs because "rap is music, not school." But she held forth on political issues in interviews. She told the *Los Angeles Times* that if she were to rap about politics, "I'd rap about some of the serious problems kids today are facing—particularly young black kids, because they don't have enough people looking out for their interests. There's that critical problem of teenage pregnancy. Kids need to be given condoms to cut down on the pregnancies. Women are in danger of losing their right to abortion—which is a horrible shame. That's really going to hurt black women in particular. Also, I think many parents—far too many black parents—are irresponsible. They don't teach their kids, don't provide the proper guidance."

This stance—calling herself apolitical while expressing very clear opinions about the intersections of race and gender—proved quite shrewd for the time. The *New York Times*'s Peter Waltrous wrote that America was "hungry for someone articulate, political and savvy about feminism but not confrontational."

Thus Latifah took a similar approach to her next two albums. On 1991's *Nature of a Sista'* she again incorporated jazz, reggae, and African rhythms into her hip-hop and included tracks such as "Latifah's Had It Up 2 Here," another song full of laying-down-the-law lyrics. ("You must learn, step, and respect the sire.") Two years later, her own Flavor Unit label partnered with Motown Records to release *Black Reign*, which included her second signature tune, "U.N.I.T.Y.," which became her most successful single.

As her musical career took off over the next few years, so did her acting career, placing Latifah among the first rappers to pivot successfully to screen, along with Will Smith, Ice T, and Ice Cube. In 1991, she appeared in Spike Lee's *Jungle Fever* and the Kid 'n Play movie *House Party 2*, as well as on TV's *The Fresh Prince of Bel-Air.* By 1993, she was starring in what would become an iconic black sitcom, *Living Single,* for which she also wrote and performed the theme song. She had her first true starring role in film with 1996's *Set It Off*, an all-female caper movie in which she played Cleo, a janitor-turned-outlaw. "There's a lot of stuff people will question about my character," she said in a *Los Angeles Times* interview. "I needed to be somebody else to show the world that I had this gift—something I can't do if I play Queen Latifah roles all of the time. I wanted to make a statement with a character who's really quite opposite of who I really am, and establish a different voice."

She got the lucrative, high-profile job of CoverGirl spokeswoman in 2001; she wasn't the first black woman to do so, but she was the most prominent. She would go on to become the brand's first spokeswoman to get her own line, the Queen Collection for women of color, who before then had a hard time finding their shades among the drugstore makeup aisle offerings.

Latifah reached peak mainstream success starring as Matron "Mama" Morton alongside Richard Gere and Catherine Zeta-Jones in 2002's Oscar-winning film version of the musical *Chicago*, for which Latifah was also nominated for an Academy Award. She took advantage of the moment to explore other forms of music, recording jazz and soul standards for her 2004 release, *The Dana Owens Album*. It did well, landing in *Billboard*'s Top 20. She could add yet another rare achievement to her résumé as a hip-hop artist who successfully transitioned to an entirely new genre. She followed up with another jazz album, *Trav'lin' Light*, in 2007, and a hip-hop album, *Persona*, in 2009. In 2015, she produced and starred in the HBO film *Bessie* as the title character, blues legend Bessie Smith.

As she has continued to tend to her empire, starring in and producing TV and movie projects as well as performing, she has found ways to keep herself balanced: she likes restorative yoga, walking, quality sleep, and staying in the moment. "Wait until next week to worry about next week," she said.

## Queen Latifah's Ancient Goddess Sister
# DANA

Latifah's given name, Dana, is fitting: Dana is the high priestess of goddesses. That is, the queen. She has divine knowledge that can help others; similarly, Latifah declared herself queen, then blazed a path for future female rappers. She shares her wisdom through writing and speaking. She serves, first and foremost, as a role model and leader. Dana, a Celtic goddess, dates back to pre-Gaelic times in Ireland when her followers were known as the Tuatha Dé Danann, "the folk of the goddess Dana," who honored her as the Creator Mother who gave life to all things. Those creatures would become what we now know as leprechauns and other Irish fairies. Queen Latifah's fans and acolytes may be even luckier than they realized.

## Invoke Queen Latifah for

Treating yourself—and acting—like a queen

Being the "first"—a pioneering woman, person of color, or member of another traditionally underrepresented group

Honoring those who came before you

## How to channel Queen Latifah's goddess energy

Study history, especially of struggles that paved the way for you to be where you are today—feminist history, Civil Rights history, gay rights history, or anything else that speaks to you.

Research and consider ways you can invest your money for the future.

Recharge so you can take on the world:
do restorative yoga, take a walk, or take a nap.

## JOURNAL RIFFS

What are you worrying about right now that you can put off worrying about (at least) until next week?

Look up the meaning of your name. Write about the ways it reflects you and/or doesn't reflect you. How has your name affected your life and identity?

How would you act differently if you were a queen? Which of those behaviors can you incorporate into your life anyway?

## power songs

"Fly Girl"
"U.N.I.T.Y."
"Ladies First"
"Fix Me, Jesus"
"I Know Where I've Been"

"He's Everything"
"Latifah's Had It Up to Here"
"Class"
"When You're Good to Mama"

"Just Another Day"
"Black Hand Side"
"Bananas (Who You Gonna Call?)"
"Dance for Me"
"Just Another Day"

# RIHANNA

## Goddess of Not Giving a Fuck

*Rapper Drake* grinned from the stage at Madison Square Garden during the 2016 MTV Video Music Awards, declaring Rihanna "someone I've been in love with since I was twenty-two years old." Rihanna, standing a few feet away in a beige satin ballgown, rolled her eyes and grimaced at the (presumably) sincere moment. Drake continued: "All my adult life I've looked up to her, even though she's younger than me. She's a living, breathing legend in our industry."

When he went to hand her the Michael Jackson Video Vanguard Award, she wasn't cowed by the moment. Drake, her rumored on-again-off-again love interest and frequent musical collaborator, went in for a passionate public kiss. She swerved right out of the way and landed on a hug. This Pop Star Goddess wasn't going to let a guy's romantic proclamations pull focus from her moment, nor allow the public spectacle to steamroll her into kissing him.

To Rihanna, international superstar Drake is just another overzealous admirer, and the MTV VMAs stage is just another day at the office.

Rihanna has dominated the pop charts since her 2005

debut album; in fact, she's the most successful artist in *Billboard*'s Pop Songs chart history, with fourteen number 1 hits as of 2019, including "We Found Love," "Work," "Umbrella," "Disturbia," "Take a Bow," "Rude Boy," and "Diamonds." (For comparison: Michael Jackson had thirteen chart-toppers, Prince had five, and Jay-Z has had four.) She's also notched an exceptional number of high-profile collaborations with the likes of Eminem ("Love the Way You Lie"), Kanye West and Paul McCartney ("FourFiveSeconds"), Jay-Z and Kanye West ("Run This Town"), and Drake ("What's My Name?," among others). She would eventually become a successful entrepreneur as well with her revolutionary Fenty Beauty makeup for all skin tones and a Fenty fashion line.

Born Robyn Rihanna Fenty on February 20, 1988, in St. Michael, Barbados, she grew up singing as an escape from her father's abuse of her mother. Her extended family, however, was so close that whenever she got a report card, she had to take it around to all her uncles and aunts so they could inspect it; if she didn't, they would come over looking for it. At fifteen, she won a high school beauty pageant, singing Mariah Carey's "Hero" during the talent portion.

Rihanna's life changed when she met U.S. record producer Evan Rogers in 2003 while he was vacationing on the island with his wife. Rihanna recorded a Caribbean-tinged pop song he wrote, "Pon de Replay," and submitted it as a demo to record labels. Thanks to that track, Jay-Z called her in to audition for his Def Jam Recordings and signed her on the spot in his New York office. The song became the then-seventeen-year-old's first hit when it was released on her 2005 album, *Music of the Sun*.

A year later, she had her first number 1 hit with "SOS," off her follow-up album, *A Girl Like Me*. But her true breakthrough came in 2007 with "Umbrella," a smash radio hit that made her a household name. It would also give Rihanna her first Grammy win in 2008.

Real life intervened in 2009. In February of that year, her then-boyfriend, R&B singer Chris Brown, beat her in their rented Lamborghini during their drive home from a pre-Grammys party.

Worse still was the aftermath: Rihanna chose, for a time, to get back together with Brown, prompting a barrage of judgmental media reactions. The public, it seemed, wanted her to play the part of the heroic survivor in a Lifetime film. Instead, she asked the court to lift the restraining order that kept Brown away from her. Later, she said in an interview that she believed at the time she could handle Brown—that, in fact, it was her special destiny to do so. "I was that girl, that girl who felt that as much pain as this relationship is, maybe some people are built stronger than others," Rihanna said. "Maybe I'm one of those people built to handle shit like this. Maybe I'm the person who's almost the guardian angel to this person, to be there when they're not strong enough, when they're not understanding the world, when they just need someone to encourage them in a positive way and say the right thing."

Rihanna did eventually end the relationship, and she went on to display her defiance in other ways. Her next album, *Rated R*, debuted a tougher persona with songs such as "Hard," "Rockstar 101," "Russian Roulette," and "Rude Boy." From "Rockstar 101": "Big shit talker / I never play the victim / I'd rather be a stalker."

She stood up for herself in business dealings, too, suing her accountants in 2012, accusing them of mishandling her money and losing millions of her dollars. It was settled in 2014 for an undisclosed amount. The next year, she coincidentally released a particularly assertive song called "Bitch Better Have My Money," which came accompanied by a video in which she kidnaps and kills the wife of a rich white man. (It also became a battle cry for beleaguered freelancers everywhere.)

By the time of her 2016 album, *Anti*, Rihanna—and her public image—had moved past the abuse. She had grown into a complicated figure with plenty else going for her: a fashion icon, an entrepreneur with a much-needed line of cosmetics for all colors and a line of lingerie for all body types, a free spirit often photographed on the street traveling from bar to bar carrying her wine right with her.

The result: the Brown incident no longer defined her. Rihanna now appeared to have more control of her career and image than ever, and she didn't give a fuck what anyone thought of her.

## Rihanna's Ancient Goddess Sister
# CHHINNAMASTA

The Hindu tradition's Chhinnamasta is, according to Sally Kempton's *Awakening Shakti*, the "goddess of radical self-transcendence"—which is spirituality-speak for being the goddess of not giving a fuck. She is not the least bit self-conscious; she lives boldly outside whatever boxes others want to put her in, how others want to see and define her. In the *Mantra Mahodadhi*, Mahidhara says, "I meditate upon the Goddess Chhinnamasta, who is seated in the centre of the Sun's disk and holds in her left hand her own severed head with gaping mouth; her hair is disheveled and she is drinking the stream of blood gushing out from her own neck." This is Rihanna unapologetically owning the spot on her journey when she was beaten by her boyfriend while refusing to be cast in a victim role because of it. This is Rihanna releasing songs like "Russian Roulette" and "S&M" after the Chris Brown incident, defiant of what a "proper victim" should be doing. This is Rihanna photographed walking out of restaurants with half-drunk wineglasses or hanging at the Grammys with a bedazzled flask. Chhinnamasta comes to us from the darkness and transforms us because of it. The headless goddess knows exactly where her head is. Being headless, she remains free from the constant chatter telling her who she should be. She does not worry about what the world thinks of her.

## Invoke Rihanna for

Standing firm in yourself in any moment, big or small

Setting boundaries

Stopping men or others in power from stealing your moment

Staying grounded

Dominating any industry you choose

Collaborating with the best in your business

## How to channel Rihanna's goddess energy

Explore what you like sexually. Many of us, especially women, don't know. For help, check out Jaclyn Friedman's book *What You Really Really Want* or fill out a yes/no/maybe list, which you can find online.

## JOURNAL RIFFS

Write about a time when you did the opposite of what was expected of you. How did it turn out? How did it feel?

How do you feel about the idea of "victimhood"? When have you felt like a victim? How did you react? Could you change your perspective and see your strength and power in the situation?

## power songs

"Work"

"Bitch Better Have My Money"

"Umbrella"

"Take a Bow"

"S&M"

"Only Girl (In the World)"

"Skin"

"Hard"

"Rockstar 101"

"Rude Boy"

"We Found Love"

"Stay"

"What's My Name?"

"FourFiveSeconds"

# SHAKIRA

## Goddess of Honoring Your Roots

*Shakira appeared* at the groundbreaking ceremony for a new school in her hometown of Barranquilla, Colombia, dropping in between stops on her 2018 world tour. She signed her autograph in the cement cornerstone, as she always did at schools she financed—a common occurrence over the previous decade-plus of her superstardom. Also as usual, she spoke of the role she believes education can play in achieving peace in her war-ravaged home country. "When some children don't receive the same education as those who live in better conditions, we can't talk about a country in peace, we can't talk about a country with equality, because education is what equalizes us," she told journalists covering the event.

As she tells it, giving back is not so much a hobby as a moral imperative. She explained to *Glamour* magazine, "Being raised in a developing country opened my eyes to so much I cannot tolerate. In Colombia, education is sometimes considered a luxury, not a human right. And it's not a priority in the agendas of many leaders. I feel a real sense of duty to use the voice and the platform I've been afforded by my fame to speak out for those whose voices don't get a chance to be heard."

Any wealthy celebrity with a conscience has adopted a pet cause, putting her power and money to good use. But Shakira's involvement with education has been long, deep, and consistent—and she is a symbol of hope to a country that has needed it after decades of civil war.

Her music similarly brings a bit of her Colombian culture to the world and intermingles it with other elements she has picked up along the way, making her work a bridge between her home country and the rest of the world. "My music, I think, is a fusion of many different elements," she told *Rolling Stone*, referencing how her performances combine such components as Andean flutes and Lebanese belly dancing. "And I'm always experimenting. So I try not to limit myself, or put myself in a category, or . . . be the architect of my own jail, you know?"

Shakira Isabel Mebarak Ripoll was born February 2, 1977, in Barranquilla, Colombia. She released two albums in her teens (*Magia* in 1991 and *Peligro* in 1993). But on 1995's *Pies Descalzos*, she came into her own as a songwriter and producer, and honed her image and sound, an Alanis Morissette–like, 1990s rock chick vibe with world music elements mixed in. *Pies Descalzos* garnered good reviews and went platinum in several Latin American countries—and it went "diamond prism" in Colombia, where she sold more than one million copies. Building on that success, she released *Dónde Están los Ladrones* in 1998. It was nominated for a Best Latin Rock Album Grammy in the United States.

The time had come to work toward a crossover in America with a record featuring English-language songs, a critical move toward international success for any artist at the time. *Laundry Service* did the trick, conquering U.S. radio in 2001 with the undeniable bop "Whenever, Wherever." (It contains such lyrical gems as, "Lucky that my breasts are small and humble / So you don't confuse them with mountains.") The soaring ballad follow-up, "Underneath Your Clothes," sealed the deal. She had perfect timing; she would become one of the marquee acts in America's Latin pop boom of the late 1990s and early 2000s (along with Ricky Martin, Enrique Iglesias, and Jennifer Lopez, who was often counted as part of the trend even though she got her start singing in English). From then on, Shakira had the money and star power to sustain an international pop career and help children in her home country get the education they need.

*Fijación Oral, Vol. 1* and *Oral Fixation, Vol. 2* in 2005 solidified her superstar status. The two-volume approach indicated she would cleverly continue to straddle both languages and markets. The Spanish-language *Fijación Oral* catered to her original fanbase and the United States's large Spanish-speaking market. *Oral Fixation* attained moderate success upon its release, but its rerelease in early 2006 contained the monster bonus track "Hips Don't Lie," which partnered Shakira with Wyclef Jean. The hit became her signature, somehow both a quintessentially Shakira song and an ode to Shakira, with Jean singing, "She makes a man wanna speak Spanish." It had undeniable staying power, as evidenced by one Internet Age moment: twelve years after "Hips Don't Lie" was released, *Goosebumps* author R. L. Stine tweeted, without context, another of Jean's lines from the song, the simplest and catchiest: "Shakira, Shakira!" It has nearly fifteen thousand retweets and thirty-eight thousand likes as of 2019.

By 2008, *Forbes* named Shakira the fourth-highest-earning woman in the music industry, topped only by the insurmountable forces that are Madonna, Barbra Streisand, and Celine Dion. Shakira's next two albums, 2009's *She Wolf* and 2010's *Sale el Sol,* showed her at the peak of her powers: the sexy empowerment of "She Wolf"; the Latin vibe on "Loca" (featuring rapper Dizzee Rascal on the English version and El Cata on the Spanish) and "Rabiosa" (featuring Pitbull on the English version and El Cata again on the Spanish); the world-music feel of "Waka Waka (This Time for Africa)," the official 2010 World Cup song. Her 2014 album, *Shakira,* demonstrated her massive cross-genre pull, featuring collaborations with country artist Blake Shelton ("Medicine") and fellow Pop Star Goddess Rihanna ("Can't Remember to Forget You").

Shakira had conquered the world. But she would never forget she was Colombian first.

## Shakira's Ancient Goddess Sister
# SEDNA

Sedna represents "infinite supply," according to Doreen Virtue's *Goddess Guidance Oracle Cards*. She preaches belief in an "abundant universe" where there is enough of everything to go around, even if outside forces have distributed it unfairly. Sedna balances giving and receiving, the key to Shakira's goddess power: because she has been so fortunate in her career, she continues to put money and effort into giving back to her home country. She does not hoard all she has been given; she shares it with the world and trusts she will always have enough. Sedna, the Inuit goddess of the sea, is also associated with bodies of water and beaches, a perfect match for Shakira, whose hometown, Barranquilla, sits on the shore of the Caribbean Sea, at the mouth of the Magdalena River.

## Invoke Shakira for

Giving back to your community
Spreading knowledge
Fighting for peace
Using your goddess powers for good
Dedicating yourself over the long term
Bridging cultures
Honoring your femininity

## How to channel Shakira's goddess energy

Choose a cause to dedicate your money and/or time to over the long haul. Make a plan to give or volunteer regularly.

Define a new territory you'd like to conquer: a new market, a new kind of job, a new hobby. Take your first steps into that crossover.

Visit the neighborhood or house where you grew up.

## JOURNAL RIFFS

What would you buy for the world if you had limitless funds?
What actions or forces would help the world move closer to peace?

## power songs

"Chantaje"
"Me Enamoré"
"Whenever, Wherever"
"Hips Don't Lie"
"Loca"

"Rabiosa"
"She Wolf"
"Ojos Así"
"Te Necesito"
"Underneath Your Clothes"

"Tú"
"Try Everything"
"Waka Waka"
"Clandestino"

## Goddess of Setting Boundaries

*A wiry* eleven-year-old girl in a beige leotard and platinum bob wig dances around a sparsely furnished room, interspersing herky-jerky modern dance moves, gorgeous ballet turns, mimed eating and drinking, and possessed-looking backbends and floor crawls. This, the video for Sia's "Chandelier," features a perfectly executed combination of modern, interpretive, and ballet dancing, evocative of cutting-edge choreographers such as Pina Bausch. In other words, it's artsy AF.

It was also an instant sensation when it premiered in 2014, featuring everything music videos are not known for: long takes instead of constant quick cuts, one set instead of several, pure talent instead of fakery. The star—dancer Maddie Ziegler—wasn't even the pop star singing the song. Ziegler became the face of the largely faceless Sia, who became a pop star in all the wrong ways, and whose star has continued to rise because of, not in spite of, her refusal to follow pop star protocol.

Maddie would go on to "play" Sia in several live performances and videos, including those for "Big Girls Cry,"

"Elastic Heart," and "Cheap Thrills." Sia had a radical idea: What if pop stars' stardom wasn't based on the way they looked? "My goal is to give girls and boys a different idea of expression," she said. "It's not always about looking pretty or cute. It's about expressing yourself however that may be, even if that's being silly or goofy or weird." What if pop stardom was based on a strong, clear voice, sonically and lyrically? Or, as Sia sings in "Bird Set Free": "I have a voice, have a voice, hear me roar tonight / You held me down / But I fought back loud."

Sia had come to a point in her career when all she wanted to do was be a songwriter, the one writing the words and tunes for others. But then she sang in a few of the tracks she wrote that became massive hits, and people grew more and more interested in her. She refused to give interviews. Somehow, this made people even more interested.

Sia Furler was born on December 18, 1975, in Adelaide, Australia. Starting at age seventeen, she sang with an acid-jazz band called Crisp until it disbanded a few years later, in 1997. She released her first solo album, *OnlySee*, that year, but it failed to make much of a commercial impact. She moved to London, where she soon got a job singing backup for British funk and acid jazz band Jamiroquai and then provided lead vocals for the electronica duo Zero 7.

In 2000, Sia again began working toward a solo career and had some success with her second full-length record, *Healing Is Difficult*. But she had problems with her record label, and a second album with a new label, 2004's *Colour*

*the Small One,* flopped. However, it also contained a ray of hope: producers of the HBO show *Six Feet Under* chose the track "Breathe Me" to accompany the show's devastating final montage, which brought renewed attention to Sia. She toured, put out a live album recorded at an April 2006 Bowery Ballroom performance called *Lady Croissant,* and recorded a fourth studio album, *Some People Have Real Problems,* which dropped in 2008. Another, *We Are Born,* came out in 2010.

Then she experienced the other side of pop success: drug and alcohol abuse. She was also diagnosed with Graves's disease, a form of hyperthyroidism that can lead to anxiety, tremors, weight loss, goiter, bulging eyes, and fatigue. She decided to abandon her solo efforts and stay in the studio, writing songs for artists including fellow Pop Star Goddesses Celine Dion, Beyoncé, and Rihanna. But even as Sia rose to hit-maker status as a songwriter, she couldn't quite stay away from singing herself. Her 2011 collaboration with French DJ David Guetta, "Titanium," became a hit based largely on her soaring vocals. She performed on the track "Elastic Heart"—with DJ Diplo and singer The Weeknd—for the *Hunger Games: Catching Fire* soundtrack in 2013.

Now she was even more in demand, a force behind the scenes and in front of the microphone. And she had one album left to deliver on her old solo contract. She decided to cautiously return to performing, this time with strict boundaries. She demanded creative control of the work and a no-promotion policy: no label-mandated interviews or appearances. She would perform publicly only in a white-blond, blunt-cut, bobbed wig with bangs so long that they covered most of her face. She didn't expect actual results from this plan. "I thought I'd shit that album out and it wouldn't do anything," she told *Rolling Stone*. "And that I would be behind the scenes from now on."

That 2014 album was *1000 Forms of Fear*, and its lead single was "Chandelier."

Starting with that song, Sia would become a pop radio staple. Starting with that video, she would cede her limelight to Maddie and her dancing whenever possible. The video, codirected by Sia, surely contributed to the song's success. Sia came up with the concept for it, then hired choreographer Ryan Heffington to iron out the details. As they were working on it, Sia (an unabashed reality-show fan) caught an episode of *Dance Moms*, on which Maddie was featured. Sia knew she wanted that girl to be in her video.

Sia eventually adapted the performance for the Grammys as well, where it stole the night with a surprise appearance from actress Kristen Wiig dancing with Maddie as Sia stood in the corner, her back to the audience, singing. "We offered something that stood out because of its content and narrative and artistic choices," Heffington explained in an interview with Vulture. "We've seen a lot of performers with backup dancers, fancy lighting, costumes, sex appeal for many, many decades, and Sia has really made a strong statement with her artistry and how she wants to portray herself and her art."

Though she continued to hide her face, her overall look—wig, giant bow, red lips—became iconic. She had found the loophole in Hollywood's obsession with appearance and sex appeal. She's the rare woman over forty who is consistently churning out hits. In *The Fader*, writer Aimee Cliff argued that Sia's stance is "changing the landscape for women in pop" and is, in fact, a feminist statement. Sia is, according to Cliff, doing performance art about pop stardom as much as she's doing pop stardom. "She's not only opting out of fame, but out of the body-scrutinizing (male) gaze that comes with that fame for so many female artists," Cliff wrote. "Sia's facelessness is political, too. We can't ignore the fact that she's a female popstar choosing to opt out of being sold on her image." Mic's Natalie Morin agreed: "Women in this industry are rarely seen as true creators; they're instead judged on everything but their music. Female musicians are constantly fighting to be noticed for something other than their image."

Sia has demonstrated feminist values in other ways as well. Fellow Pop Star Goddess Adele told *Rolling Stone* about working with Sia on her album *25*. "I actually love the dynamic of us both being in there and just fucking being bossy," Adele said. "And it's all these male producers, and they're all fucking shitting themselves 'cause we're in there." Sia responded to that description in a separate interview: "It's funny because both of us are quite dominant because we are both skillful at our jobs of songwriting or singing. I think that maybe we're not dominant but confident. I think because we're both very confident in our skills, we're just naturally alpha in some way in terms of our work."

Sia occasionally appears in public without the wig at show-business parties or while conducting regular-person business like catching a plane. But she retains her bewigged persona for anything performance-related, including her side project with UK soul singer Labrinth and DJ/producer Diplo, LSD.

To continue her solo success, she has been forced to drop another aversion besides fame: an aversion to unapologetic pop music. She described her own hits to *Rolling Stone* as "terribly, terribly cheesy." She didn't even listen to pop music until she started writing it. The title of her 2016 album, *This Is Acting,* points to both this reluctance and the album's concept—it is a collection of songs she's written for other artists but which were rejected. (Sia wrote "Cheap Thrills" and "Reaper," for instance, for Rihanna.)

Sia wants to give you the pleasures of pop without wrecking herself for the star part, making her a new kind of Pop Star Goddess. And it seems, against all pop music convention, to be working.

## Sia's Ancient Goddess Sister
# ISHTAR

Babylonian goddess Ishtar represents setting boundaries, according to Doreen Virtue's *Goddess Guidance Oracle Cards*—saying no as an act of self-care, just as Sia has set clear limits on what she will and will not do for pop stardom. While we love our other goddesses for all they give, many have experienced dangerous breakdowns under the pressure of stardom. Sia likely still gets tired, irritated, and overworked, but she has found an ingenious way to cut back on negative energy. In the wake of her own breakdown, she managed to gain enough perspective to see a new way through. And she has been remarkably assertive—and creative—in executing that vision. Ishtar gives us an image of womanhood that goes against more modern, Western ideals of womanhood that require endless giving of oneself, just as Sia gives us a new image of the female pop star.

## Invoke Sia for

Saying no when you need to

Embracing art, high and low

Reconceiving your vision for your job, career, or life roles

## How to channel Sia's goddess energy

Delegate tasks you don't want to do so you can focus
on the ones you do want to do.

Experiment with wigs or outlandish accessories.

Give yourself permission to be "bossy" for a day and see what happens.

## JOURNAL RIFFS

In what areas of your life do you need to set more boundaries?
How can you start doing that?

Write about a time when you broke down under pressure. What can
you do differently in the future to prevent that from happening?

What role in your life (your job position, or as a wife/mother/sister/friend)
needs to be overhauled? What are some creative ways to reenvision it?

## power songs

"Alive"

"Cheap Thrills"

"Breathe Me"

"Chandelier"

"Big Girls Cry"

"Elastic Heart"

"The Greatest"

"Bird Set Free"

"Unstoppable"

"I'm Still Here"

"One Million Bullets"

"Move Your Body"

"Reaper"

"House on Fire"

# SOLANGE

## Goddess of Finding Your Own Path

*Solange turned in* her third album, 2016's *A Seat at the Table*, seventy-two hours before its scheduled release. She felt nauseated: "There was a lot of fear and emotion, pain and hurt and rage," she told *Glamour*, because the work was meant to express and release the fact that she was "carrying around so many microaggressions that transitioned into trauma, that transitioned into rage, that transitioned into a weight I carried around."

She sent in the mastered tracks from her new chosen home of New Orleans, where her sister, Beyoncé, happened to be at the time, filming her own video. Solange later explained: "I think I felt like the minute I turned it in, there would be this sort of lightness to come immediately—this erasure of all those things that I had worked through during the writing process. But it didn't come. I realized I needed a second to remove myself from everything, to feel my connection to the album without everyone's voices."

She said to her husband, "Let's go to Mexico!" Then she turned off her phone and went. A few days later, she turned her phone back on. Her manager had texted her a screenshot of the cover of her album hovering at the top of the iTunes chart. She had her first major hit record. It would debut at number 1 on the *Billboard* chart and go on to win a Grammy for Best R&B Performance for the single "Cranes in the Sky."

Solange had enjoyed moderate novelty success as Beyoncé's little sister with 2002's *Solo Star* and critical acclaim with 2008's *Sol-Angel and the Hadley St. Dreams.* But *A Seat at the Table* proved she was a distinct force in her own right, which would continue at least through 2019's *When I Get Home.*

Solange Piaget Knowles was born June 24, 1986, in Houston, Texas, to Matthew and Tina Knowles. In 2001, she got her big break at fifteen, writing and singing the theme song for the Disney Channel show *The Proud Family* with her sister's group, Destiny's Child. *Solo Star* came out a year later, but Solange's personal life soon pulled her attention away from her career. She married boyfriend Daniel Smith in 2004 when she was seventeen and he was nineteen; she gave birth to their son eight months later, and Solange confirmed their divorce three years later. She tried acting, first in 2004's *Johnson Family Vacation* and then in 2006 with *Bring It On: All or Nothing.*

In a "letter to her teenage self" in *Teen Vogue*, Solange described the early stages of her life: "the dance-is-life (aka 'this leotard is my second skin') phase, the Bible-thumping-church-camp phase (which coincided and contradicted with the Fiona-Apple-fan-club-president phase), the Nas-aficionado-brown-lip-liner-and-Vaseline phase, the Rasta-vegan-thrifter-who-is-determined-to-marry-Brandon-Boyd phase, the football-player's-girlfriend-who-wears-braided-blond-highlights-and-swears-by-capri-pants phase."

She continued: "sometimes you push these phases to the max, and when you go out into the world feeling confident in who you are and what you reflect, young folks will call you names and grown folks will call you names. It's ok. one day you will name yourself, and that name will belong to you."

Solange got out from under Beyoncé's shadow, no small accomplishment; most of us are still living there (happily), and we don't even know her personally. But in the case of Solange, it was a superhuman feat. Everything in her young life revolved around her sister. She worked as a backup dancer for Beyoncé's group, Destiny's Child. Their success undoubtedly helped Solange secure the *Proud Family* theme-song gig. Her status as Beyoncé's sister lent her entrée into the music business and gave her curiosity appeal, but also made it much harder for anyone to take her art seriously. She made some headway with her acclaimed 2008 album *Sol-Angel and the Hadley St. Dreams*, with a sound that recalled Motown girl groups.

But then in 2014, Solange became an instant legend— for gossipy reasons once again linked to her sister. Leaked security camera footage showed Solange yelling at, punching, and kicking Beyoncé's husband, rapper Jay-Z, in an elevator after the annual high-fashion Met Gala. The rumored cause: Jay-Z's infidelity, later acknowledged through Beyoncé's *Lemonade* and Jay-Z's *4:44*.

Even Solange's creative breakthrough, *A Seat at the Table,* had to share the spotlight with her sister's masterpiece, *Lemonade*; Solange's album came out five months after that showstopper.

Yet Solange learned to see Beyoncé's presence in her life as an advantage, telling her sister in an *Interview* magazine exchange that it gave her lots of "practice" in following her own inspiration. "Growing up in a household with a master class such as yourself definitely didn't hurt," Solange told Beyoncé. "And, as far back as I can remember, our mother always taught us to be in control of our voice and our bodies and our work, and she showed us that through her example. If she conjured up an idea, there was not one element of that idea that she was not going to have her hand in."

This led both women to control their own output and image, no easy task when you're young and female and working in the music industry: "It's something I've learned so much about from you, getting to be in control of your own narrative," Solange said to Beyoncé. "And, at this point, it should be an expectation, not something that you're asking permission for."

Still, she said, she struggled with an issue many young women struggle with, talking herself up. "One thing that I constantly have to fight against is not feeling arrogant when I say I wrote every lyric on this album. I still have not been able to say that. That's the first time I've actually ever said it, because of the challenges that we go through when we celebrate our work and our achievements."

With *A Seat at the Table*, she became a leading voice for black women in pop culture. "Solange represents in her work the story of black life yesterday, today, and tomorrow and the indomitable spirit of black women," Thelma Golden, the director and chief curator of the Studio Museum in Harlem, wrote in *Teen Vogue*. "In a culture that has often defined beauty so narrowly and placed so many limitations on possibility, she shows us that we need not accept others' projections of who we are. Instead, we will boldly exist at the creations of our own powerful imaginations, redefining beauty and possibility without limits, knowing and loving who we are."

Of course, that comes with irritations, insults, public battles, and worse. The *London Evening Standard*, for instance, digitally removed Solange's braids from an image on its cover in 2017, an act for which it later apologized. The photo accompanied a piece in which she talked about the important African American cultural legacy of hair braiding and *A Seat at the Table*, which includes the song "Don't Touch My Hair."

She has continued her activism unabated. She performed at the Peace Ball in 2017, an alternative to the inauguration balls thrown for President Donald Trump, held at the National Museum of African American History and Culture. Solange was introduced by legendary Civil Rights activist Angela Davis, who said: "Certainly in our resistance, we need art. We need music. We need poetry. . . . Now, you are about to witness a performance by one who will help us to produce the anthems of our resistance." Solange spoke at a Yale conference about the importance of activism in pop music. She has also paid tribute to a number of black female artists: introducing Erykah Badu at an Essence Black Women in Music event in 2017, celebrating writer Zora Neale Hurston in a BBC Radio 4 documentary in 2017, wearing a full-length puffer jacket dress at the 2017 Met Gala to evoke fellow Pop Star Goddess Missy Elliott's iconic trash-bag suit in the 1997 video for "The Rain (Supa Dupa Fly)." Solange created a digital art installation called "Seventy States" that appeared at the Tate Modern in London as part of its *Soul of a Nation: Art in the Age of Black Power* exhibit in 2017. Her 2019 album, *When I Get Home,* as critically revered as *A Seat at the Table,* solidified her place as a musical activist on behalf of women and African Americans.

Solange is more than Beyoncé's sister. She is more than a pop star. She is an artist and an activist, exactly what the world needs now.

## Solange's Ancient Goddess Sister
# BASTET

Bastet represents independence as a route to success, just as Solange's quest to define herself apart from her famous sister led to her unique and highly regarded artistic expressions. Solange often speaks about the importance of reflection and solitude in her creative process, and the difficulties of the traditional pop star cycle (record, tour, repeat); Bastet helps to balance extroversion and introversion, public-facing endeavors and private time. Also like Bastet, Solange has taken control of her career and creative output, serving as the final word on all her projects. Bastet, an Egyptian goddess and daughter of sun god Ra, acquires these qualities by turning into a cat—the most independent of domestic animals—every night. She exhibits grace, playfulness, and intuition.

## Invoke Solange for

Forging a unique path in your industry or artistry

Processing microaggressions

Being a good sister

## How to channel Solange's goddess energy

Plan a quick (or not-so-quick) getaway where
you can unplug from work and life.

Tell your siblings, family members, or friends how they've inspired you.

Celebrate your most recent achievement, large or small.

## JOURNAL RIFFS

How can you be a better sibling, child, parent, partner, or friend?

If you could go anywhere to shut out the world, where would you go?

What is an uncharted territory that you can explore
in your art or profession?

## power songs

"Dancing in the Dark"
"Cranes in the Sky"
"Mad"
"Don't Touch My
  Hair"
"Weary"
"Losing You"

"Some Things Never
  Seem to Fucking
  Work"
"Locked in Closets"
"Lovers in the Parking
  Lot"
"Don't Let Me Down"

"Bad Girls"
"Rise"
"Almeda"
"Stay Flo"
"Binz"

## Goddess of Powerful Vulnerability

*SZA had* been so low on cash that she pretended to be vegan, surviving on chips, avocado, and salad mix. She was twenty-six and her first full-length studio album, *Ctrl,* was about to be released. In lower moments, she had begged her record label president, Terrence "Punch" Henderson, to assign writers to work on her album because she didn't trust her own writing—"I thought no one would ever like me the way I was," she later wrote in a social media post. He told her, "You don't need them."

When *Ctrl* was nominated for five Grammys in 2017, SZA reflected on this time in an emotional Instagram post: "never gave my parents an opportunity to say 'wow my kids killing it' didn't graduate or do any fly shit before my nana died . been fired from every job I ever had .I remember sobbing on the phone w punch pleading for the album not to come out cause I couldn't take the embarrassment . Just wanted another week . Another day ?.he ignored me n said I'd be fine . . . This entire thing puts my wildest dreams to shame."

In many ways an antigoddess, SZA never pretends she has superhuman confidence when she doesn't; she is loath to wear anything uncomfortable. She says things like, "I feel like every outfit I have ever planned ahead is trash."

These kinds of thoughts—self-denigrating, raw, vulnerable—have made her a standout in her young career. *Ctrl* sticks close to its stated theme: giving up the fantasy that as humans we control things. On the song "Prom" she sings: "Am I doin' enough? / Feel like I'm wastin' time." On "Normal Girl": "I really wish I was a normal girl, oh my / How do I be, how do I be a lady?" On "20 Something": "Prayin' the 20 somethings don't kill me, don't kill me . . ."

The record also includes, charmingly, audio clips of advice from her mother and grandmother—the subtext being that SZA doesn't have all the answers. One has her grandmother addressing her by her birth name: "Solána, if you don't say something, speak up for yourself, they think you stupid, you know what I'm saying?" Her mother, Audrey, underlining the concept of the album, says: "We take things, and my influence, so far, and then it's out of my hands. And, you know, while as I said it can be scary, it can also be a little bit comforting. Because I've learned that when I get to that point . . . I can acknowledge, 'Okay, Audrey, that's as much as you can do,' I can actually let it go."

SZA told *Time* magazine the two women represented different perspectives in her own life and on the album: "I think I got my obsession with control from her [my mom]. My granny is salty and sweet . . . [she] is much more like me, while my mother is just like, the sweetest, most pure."

SZA was born Solána Imani Rowe on November 8, 1990, in St. Louis, and was raised in Maplewood, New Jersey. She grew up Muslim but stopped wearing her hijab after 9/11. She's described her parents as "conservative" and "traditional" people who listened to John Coltrane and Miles Davis, which would eventually influence her own music. But in her teens, she branched out into Limp Bizkit, Red Hot Chili Peppers, Macy Gray, and Nine Inch Nails. She became interested in singing professionally when her brother, a rapper, asked her to serve as the hook girl on his mixtape.

She came up with her stage name (pronounced phonetically: *siz-uh*) as an acronym derived from the Supreme Alphabet of the Five-Percent Nation, a splinter group of the Nation of Islam founded in Harlem in the 1960s. In the Supreme Alphabet, *S* stands for "sovereign," *Z* stands for "zigzag," and *A* stands for "Allah." She put together two self-released mixtapes, and at a party in 2011, a friend passed her demo along to Punch Henderson, president of Top Dawg Entertainment (or TDE, best known for representing Kendrick Lamar, who was performing at the party—a party SZA's boyfriend's clothing company sponsored). In 2013, she became the first woman to be signed to TDE, which released her EP *Z*. Critics deemed it promising, but not yet cohesive.

Media anticipation for her work only increased her insecurities, even as far back as the 2014 release of *Z*. "My pressure doesn't really come from music, my pressure comes from everything else, the things that are just part of being a 'public figure,'" she said in a Huffington Post interview. "Everyone has an opinion on you and thinks they know you or what you're trying to do."

Her image caused her even more stress: "The fact that I'm a fuller-figured, brown-skinned woman with curly hair now means that I must be striving for Erykah Baduism, part two, because I could never be part one," she said. "But I have no desire to be that. As amazing of an artist as she is, I don't want to be pigeonholed into the being of someone else or something. I just want to be able to do what I want to do."

Three years later, she did just that, and reaped rewards. *Ctrl* charmed critics and sold well. The *New York Times*'s Jon Pareles said that with *Ctrl* SZA "has found herself a sector of what's often called alt-R&B or future R&B: a meditative refuge from aggressive beats and unsubtle hooks, and a place for experiments that have gradually and stealthily infiltrated more mainstream pop. . . . Her voice is upfront, recorded to sound natural and unaffected, with all its grain and conversational quirks. And the album begins and ends with songs that back her with a guitar and little else, a signal of unadorned openness." It debuted at number 3 on the *Billboard* chart and went platinum in the United States.

Those five Grammy nominations made SZA the most-nominated woman that year. She ultimately went home with no statues, stoking years-long outrage about sexism and racism pervading the awards show. (Jay-Z also left empty-handed that year.) The same year, she also received the "Rule Breaker" award at the Billboard Women in Music celebration—a less prestigious accolade, but certainly an apt one.

Like other Pop Star Goddesses of her generation, SZA has shared an extraordinary amount with her fans via social media. Her tweets extend the spirit of her lyrics. Case in point, from her Twitter feed: "I just want my booty rubbed and a moderate amount of attention." Another time, she tweeted with no context: "Wish I meant more to u." Don't worry, she cheered up two weeks later: "Yo this blood moon retrograde tried me but I can faithfully say I beat its ass." Then there's: "I need one uh those nervous tags they put on dogs that can't deal?" And just: "Regret."

And finally: "I'm not brave everyday but when I am its LIFE CHANGING! PLEASE DON'T WAIT TO GET OUT OF UR HEADS !! SAY WHAT U WANT NOW !! BE WHO U ARE NOW ! BE BRAVE EVERYDAY ! THE TINIEST BIT GOES A LONG WAY I PROMISE! FUCK OPINIONS! THE RISKS IS WORTH IT. I LOVE YOU. I BELIEVE IN YOU."

Oh, wait, one more: "Look in the mirror. Figure out what u need. Give it to urself."

SZA's Ancient Goddess Sister

# BHERUNDA NITYA

The fifteen Nityas correspond to different phases of the moon and represent variations on the yogic goddess Lalita. Bherunda is the Nitya of vulnerability, who shows up when the moon is crescent-shaped. She has three eyes and eight arms, with a body the color of molten gold. Ready to protect herself and others, she holds a noose, sword, thunderbolt, bow, and arrow; most importantly, she has a shield that works like an incantation, a protective spell one could sing. Naked except for her gold jewelry, she dissolves the "poisons" of fear and shame by exposing herself. SZA, a close watcher of moon phases herself, has triumphed by sharing her own most vulnerable moments and inspires others to embrace their own "flaws" by acknowledging her own.

## Invoke SZA for

Pushing through moments of self-doubt

Admitting your weaknesses and mistakes

Having hope in your worst moments

Living in the moment

Feeling the power of vulnerability

Letting go of control

Surviving your twenties

## How to channel SZA's goddess energy

Ask for advice from your elders—
mother, grandmother, other older women.

Find one issue in your life to just let go of, to let what happens happen.

Consider sharing your lesser moments and feelings as well as
your perfect moments and feelings on social media.

## JOURNAL RIFFS

What do you need or want most right now?

Do some research to find out what phase the moon is in and what energies
it might represent. Write about your reactions.
How can you best take advantage of those energies?

## power songs

"Love Galore"

"The Weekend"

"All the Stars"

"Garden (Say It Like
Dat)"

"Broken Clocks"

"Supermodel"

"Doves in the Wind"

"Drew Barrymore"

"Go Gina"

"Normal Girl"

"Anything"

"Prom"

"20 Something"

# TAYLOR SWIFT

## Goddess of Demanding Your Worth

*Taylor Swift* sits at home in her New York City apartment, cuddling on the sofa with her two cats: Olivia Benson, a fluffy, white, smushy-faced Scottish Fold; and Meredith Grey, a gray and white, angry-faced Scottish Fold. She named both of them for great female TV characters, because Taylor loves watching TV—especially *Friends* reruns—with them.

Taylor Swift has described this as her ideal at-rest scenario.

It also reflects Taylor Swift's goddess essence: she is the regular girl with ideas of gold—and the guts to demand their worth. Throughout her career as a country star and then a pop idol, no matter how glamorous her life has gotten, she's continued to play back to her roots as a basic suburban girl with intense feelings that she just happens to spin into catchy, chart-topping hits.

She was born in Reading, Pennsylvania, in 1989, to Scott, a financial adviser, and Andrea, a former marketing executive for a mutual fund. Taylor spent her youth on the family Christmas tree farm in Pennsylvania, along with her younger brother, Austin. She's journaled for most of her life, always dealing with her emotions by writing about them. Many of her scribblings—romantic, longing, angsty, vengeful—would become massive hits.

Thus Taylor's life experiences have always formed the basis of her work, as she grew from writing songs about boys in her class to dropping lyrical hints about the famous men she has dated, including actor Jake Gyllenhaal, singer Harry Styles, and actor Tom Hiddleston. This transition has served her well, having the effect of turning these major male stars into mere mortals from Taylor's diary, rather than making her seem impossibly famous and glamorous to the fans who relate to her so strongly.

As her real life has grown more removed from regular people's lives, she has bridged this age-old singer-songwriter dilemma better than anyone else. That is, if by "better" you mean "more profitably."

When Taylor was fourteen years old, her family relocated to a suburb of Nashville so she could pursue her songwriting dreams. She soon signed a contract to write for Sony/ATV Nashville, a deal that made her the youngest-ever pro songwriter for country music's major publishing outfit. A year later she made a deal as a performer with an upstart label called Big Machine Records, which put out her first album, *Taylor Swift,* in 2006.

The record was born of her personal motto from the time, a favorite line from the 2003 romantic comedy *Love Actually,* the kind of sentiment that seems profound in your adolescent haze: "If you look around, love actually *is* all around." The tracks were soaked in the syrupy feelings of first loves and heartbreaks, the never-ending waves of emotions that mark typical teenage years. The album won her instant, passionate fans for good reason: "Teenage girls, especially, are taught that many of their feelings and thoughts are silly, insignificant, and shallow. It's into those frequently shameful anxieties that Taylor Swift has pried," wrote Caitlin PenzeyMoog for the A.V. Club.

As Taylor and her loves grew more famous, however, her honest approach to songwriting made her the subject of jokes that painted her as a love-crazed, fairy-tale-obsessed lunatic careening about Hollywood. Taylor shot back in an interview: "For a female to write about her feelings, and then be portrayed as some clingy, insane, desperate girlfriend in need of making you marry her and have kids with her . . . I think that's taking something that potentially should be celebrated—a woman writing about her feelings in a confessional way—and turning it and twisting it into something that is frankly a little sexist."

These kinds of attacks on Taylor invigorated her fanbase, who saw her as a friend and jumped to defend her. She reciprocated, to an extraordinary degree. She held a listening party at her own apartment for some fans when her album *1989* came out. She made and sent individual Christmas care packages to fans. She has paid off fans' student loans and covered their medical costs, crashed their bridal showers, baked cookies with them, and given lots of individual, personal advice on Instagram.

Many of those fans discovered her in her teen country phase, but they followed as she transitioned from country to pop with her 2012 album, *Red*. Two years later, she went full pop with *1989*, and her fans remained as obsessed as ever, even as she embraced the pop star life by moving into a nearly $20 million New York City apartment.

Her fans always saw her as that regular girl, no matter what. But as time went by, her famous exes and other stars began to see her differently.

Taylor does have a goddess shadow side.

She once said, "Silence speaks so much louder than screaming tantrums. Never give anyone an excuse to say that you're crazy." This policy would come to haunt her during her most trying times, as she stayed quiet at the wrong times and clumsily went on the attack at the wrong times throughout a number of high-profile feuds with other celebrities.

She took even more heat for staying mum during the contentious 2016 election for U.S. president as many other celebrities campaigned for Hillary Clinton, including some of her biggest pop rivals. When Taylor finally made her first political statement, endorsing Democratic congressional candidates in her home state of Tennessee during the 2018 midterm elections, she proved she could move the needle by breaking her silence. More than 169,000 new voters registered in the forty-eight hours after her October 8 endorsement, nearly three times the number who registered in all of August. A disproportionate number of registrations came from young people and from Tennessee, indicating that she had, indeed, made quite a difference—and perhaps could have done the same during the crucial 2016 presidential election.

Taylor maintained a form of silence even when it came to her own love life, which she used as material for songs and then declined to elaborate on in interviews. This only resulted in more media scrutiny of her personal life. She fed the frenzy by offering up clues in the songs and videos. Was the reference to "two paper airplanes flying" a hint that "Out of the Woods" was about Harry Styles, who gave her a paper plane necklace? Was the discarded diamond engagement ring in the "Look What You Made Me Do" video a hint that DJ Calvin Harris had proposed, and she had said no? Taylor's passive-aggressive communication style turned out to be tinder for a bonfire of conspiracy-theory-level speculation—and a major driver of her popularity.

However, she couldn't control this force as much as she might have liked. Paparazzi followed her everywhere. In 2014, she publicly swore off dating. She retreated into her friendships with other high-profile women like supermodels Gigi Hadid and Karlie Kloss, singer-actress Selena Gomez, and auteur Lena Dunham, often bringing them onstage with her during concerts and creating the viral idea of #squadgoals. But many saw these public displays as exclusionary, Taylor flaunting her wealthy, famous, mostly white friends in the name of fake feminism.

Taylor found herself in a phase when everything she did seemed to go the wrong way. Her blond, willowy looks earned her a following among Nazis online as an "Aryan goddess"—not the kind of goddess we're talking about in this book. Her penchant for holding grudges—and commenting on them only via her songs and videos—blew up in a number of legendary feuds. A fight with fellow pop star Katy Perry, reportedly over backup dancers, was supposedly the inspiration for Taylor's song "Bad Blood"; it in turn spawned a high-budget, sci-fi battle showdown video featuring Taylor's famous friends. (The two recently reconciled in Taylor's "You Need to Calm Down" video.) Taylor then got into a Twitter tussle with Nicki Minaj when Nicki complained about "Bad Blood," featuring "very slim" white women, getting an MTV Video Music Award nomination when Nicki's own "Anaconda" did not. Taylor eventually apologized, saying she hadn't understood Nicki's beef was with MTV for its exclusion of black women, not with Taylor herself, but the incident didn't help combat Taylor's reputation as self-centered.

One of Taylor's more admirable qualities—her desire to be properly credited for her accomplishments—seemed to cause unexpected blowback and compound negative public perception of her during this time. (Perhaps due to the resiliency of the patriarchy and internalized misogyny?) This supposedly even contributed to her breakup with Calvin Harris in 2016. She ghost-wrote his hit with Rihanna, "This Is What You Came For," and while promoting it, Harris told an interviewer he couldn't imagine ever collaborating with Taylor. Apparently that denial was a bit too heavy-handed, and they broke up soon afterward. Her team then revealed that Taylor was, in fact, behind the credited pseudonym, Nils Sjoberg.

Taylor traded public jabs on and off for years with rapper Kanye West, starting with his infamous interruption of her acceptance speech at the 2009 VMAs ("I'mma let you finish . . .") and hitting a new, explosive high when he dropped her name in his song "Famous": "I feel like me and Taylor might still have sex / Why? I made that bitch famous." She shot back in a 2016 Grammy acceptance speech, in which she pointed to a telling portion of the lines—but not the bit about them having sex and not even about him calling her a "bitch." Rather, she said: "I want to say to all the young women out there: There are going to be people along the way who will try to undercut your success or take credit for your accomplishments or your fame," she said. "But if you just focus on the work and you don't let those people sidetrack you, someday when you get where you're going, you'll look around and you will know that it was you and

the people who love you who put you there."

In true Swiftian form, soon afterward she gathered up all her worst moments and tendencies and put them into song and video form: her 2017 hit "Look What You Made Me Do" is either brilliant self-parody, the height of self-indulgence, or a lot of both. She makes clear references in the song and video to Kanye, Katy, and Calvin. In an embarrassingly on-the-nose interlude, she says, "I'm sorry, the old Taylor can't come to the phone right now. Why? Oh, 'cause she's dead." She ends the video with representations of fourteen different personae she's embodied throughout her career, from naive and nerdy to a hissing snake-charmer (a reference to #taylorswiftisasnake memes hinted at on social media by West's wife, Kim Kardashian West).

Then again, Taylor's vengeful, exacting dark side has done some good as well. She's resisted making her music available for streaming services concurrent with its release—in other words, she has demanded to be paid full price for her albums, despite the popularity of streaming. And they became huge hits in actual CD and download sales. She defended her position in a *Wall Street Journal* op-ed: "In my opinion, the value of an album is, and will continue to be, based on the amount of heart and soul an artist has bled into a body of work, and the financial value that artists (and their labels) place on their music when it goes out into the marketplace."

She also sued a Denver radio personality, David Mueller, for sexual assault, saying he groped her during a photo op at an event. In August 2017, she won a moral victory (and a symbolic $1, the amount she sued for) after confidently testifying. When asked why the front of her skirt wasn't rumpled in the photo from Mueller's attack, she answered, "Because my ass is located at the back of my body." When asked by Mueller's lawyer how she felt about Mueller losing his job over the incident, she responded, "I'm not going to let you or your client make me feel in any way that this is my fault. Here we are years later, and I'm being blamed for the unfortunate events of his life that are the product of his decisions—not mine."

Taylor maintains unwavering confidence in her worth. When she was growing up, she wanted to be a financial adviser like her father. Perhaps he taught her to demand what she deserves. She knows all the lyrics to Kendrick Lamar's "Backseat Freestyle." It begins: "All my life I want money and power."

Now she has it, and she isn't afraid to use it to tell her truth, speak her mind, or demand more.

## Taylor's Ancient Goddess Sister
# SESHAT

Taylor's ascent would please Seshat, the Egyptian goddess of wisdom, knowledge, writing, and, in some tellings, accounting and math. Seshat is known for her expertise, as scribes were highly prized for their rare language skills. She's often depicted marking the passage of time on a palm stem, something Taylor would surely appreciate; her lyrics return over and over to beginnings, endings, the poignant impermanence of relationships, and the mysteries of aging. But Seshat and Taylor would likely bond most over the power of writing—and accounting, the financial kind *and* the score-settling kind.

## Invoke Taylor for

Asking for a raise
Managing your money
Investing
Putting your heart and soul into your work
Valuing your own thoughts and feelings
Standing up for yourself

## How to channel Taylor's goddess energy

Journal about your goals, your monetary dreams, and your
plans for achieving them.

Stay home with your cats or binge-watch *Friends* (or your favorite
equivalents) when you need to recharge. You'll need energy to
go out into the world and fight for what you deserve.

## JOURNAL RIFFS

How much money do you want to make? What's your plan for getting it?
Write your thoughts, whatever they are, for three pages without stopping.
Don't censor yourself. Later, go back and look for the nuggets of gold.
If there aren't any, that's okay, too. Just do it again tomorrow, and the next
day, and the next day. There's value in hearing and honoring
your own thoughts and feelings.

## power songs

"Blank Space"
"Speak Now"
"Picture to Burn"
"Bad Blood"
". . . Ready for It?"
"Fearless"
"Lover"

"Shake It Off"
"We Are Never
    Ever Getting Back
    Together"
"Better Than
    Revenge"
"Don't Blame Me"

"Mean"
"You Belong with Me"
"The Man"
"This Is Why We Can't
    Have Nice Things"

# ACKNOWLEDGMENTS

*Thank you* to my agent, Laurie Abkemeier, for picking this idea out of a long list of book ideas I had come up with but thought were way too fun for anyone to actually pay me for; to my editor, Emma Brodie, for paying me for it and being such an enthusiastic cheerleader; to Robin Markle for the killer illustrations; and to Britney, Beyoncé, and the rest of the goddesses for inspiring me and so many others.

# SOURCES

A special thanks to the following two sources, which are referenced throughout this book:

Kempton, Sally. *Awakening Shakti: The Transformative Power of the Goddesses of Yoga.* Boulder, Colorado: Sounds True, 2013.

Virtue, Doreen. *Guidebook for the Goddess Guidance Oracle Cards.* Carlsbad, California: Hay House, Inc., 2004.

## ADELE

Adams, Guy. "Straight in at No. 1 . . . America embraces Adele, the 'Anti-Gaga.'" *Independent,* March 5, 2011.

"Adele's Health Crisis and Comeback." *People,* February 8, 2012.

Barrett, Christopher. "The Adele Experience." *M Magazine,* May 10, 2011.

D'Souza, Christa. "Adele Cover Interview." *British Vogue,* October 2011.

Husband, Stuart. "Adele: Young Soul Rebel." *Telegraph,* April 27, 2008.

Lansky, Sam. "Adele Is Music's Past, Present and Future." *Time,* December 21, 2015.

Lewis, Pete. "Adele: Up Close and Personal." *Blues & Soul,* Issue 1092 (2008).

Touré. "Adele Opens Up About Her Inspirations, Looks, and Stage Fright." *Rolling Stone,* April 28, 2011.

Willman, Chris, and Robert Levine. "Does Adele's Historic Sales Performance Mark a Turning Point for the Music Industry? A Debate." *Billboard,* December 10, 2015.

*Your World with Neil Cavuto.* "Grammy Wins by Adele, Clarkson Fuel New Debate Over Weight." Fox News, February 11, 2013.

### ALICIA KEYS

Beusman, Callie. "For Chrissake, Going Without Makeup Is Neither a Trend Nor Laziness." Jezebel, April 17, 2014.

Bouwman, Kimbel. "Interview with Peter Edge, A&R at J Records for Alicia Keys, Dido, Angie Stone." HitQuarters.com, October 13, 2004.

Elan, Priya. "Why Alicia Keys' #nomakeup Look Is Not Quite as 'Real' as It Seems." *Guardian,* October 10, 2016.

Freedman, Jared. "Alicia Keys." Citizens of Humanity online magazine, July 6, 2016.

Keys, Alicia. "Alicia Keys: Time to Uncover." Lenny Letter, May 31, 2016.

Larkworthy, Jane. "Meet the Woman Behind Alicia Keys' No Makeup Look and Glowing Complexion." *W,* October 5, 2016.

Merritt, Stephanie. "Soul Sister Number One." *Guardian,* March 21, 2004.

Philbrook, Erik. "Alicia Keys—A Legend Grows." ASCAP.com, June 1, 2005.

Saraiya, Sonia. "Alicia Keys: Why Women Need to 'Infiltrate Our Industries' to Shift the Power Balance." *Variety,* April 10, 2018.

### ARIANA GRANDE

Leight, Elias. "Some Albums Take Years. Ariana Grande Made 'Thank U, Next' in 2 Weeks." *Rolling Stone,* February 9, 2019.

McLean, Craig. "Ariana Grande: 'If you want to call me a diva I'll say: cool.'" *Telegraph,* October 17, 2014.

### BEYONCÉ

*Life Is But a Dream.* Directed by Ed Burke and Beyoncé Knowles. New York: ICM Partners and Parkwood Entertainment, 2013.

### BRITNEY SPEARS

"Britney Spears: Biography." RollingStone.com. Archived from the original, retrieved August 16, 2019.

Grigoriadis, Vanessa. "The Tragedy of Britney Spears." *Rolling Stone,* February 21, 2008.

*I Am Britney Jean.* Directed by Fenton Bailey and Randy Barbato, Los Angeles: World of Wonder, 2013.

Schwarz, Hunter. "The Secret History of Britney Spears' Lost Album." BuzzFeed, April 27, 2014.


## CARDI B

Elan, Priya. "The Best Albums of 2018, No. 4: Cardi B—*Invasion of Privacy.*" *Guardian,* December 18, 2018.

Ellis-Petersen, Hannah. "The New American Dream: Cardi B's Rise from Instagram to Chart-Topping Rapper." *Guardian,* September 29, 2017.

Estevez, Marjua. "Cardi B Doesn't Give a F**k, and Neither Should You." *Vibe,* November 15, 2016.

*Jimmy Kimmel Live!* ABC, October 17, 2018.

Madden, Sidney. "The Business of Being Cardi B." NPR's *The Record,* April 5, 2018.

Nikas, Joanna. "An Afternoon with Cardi B as She Makes Money Moves." *New York Times,* August 17, 2017.

Weaver, Caity. "Cardi B's Money Moves." *GQ,* April 9, 2018.


## CARLA BRUNI

Brown, Helen. "Carla Bruni Interview: '10 years with my husband has been a miracle.'" *Telegraph,* October 7, 2017.

Brown, Helen. "Review: Carla Bruni's New Album." *Telegraph,* July 9, 2008.

Heyman, Marshall. "Carla Bruni Uncensored." *Harper's Bazaar,* August 30, 2017.

Hoggard, Liz. "Carla Bruni, No Promises." *Guardian,* April 21, 2007.

Salmon, Caspar. "Carla Bruni: *No Promises.*" AllMusic, retrieved August 16, 2019.

Thomas, Dana. "Carla Bruni-Sarkozy: Me and My Guitar." *New York Times,* October 3, 2017.

Trebay, Guy. "The French President's Lover." *New York Times,* January 13, 2008.

### CARLY RAE JEPSEN

Acuna, Kirsten. "Pop Star Carly Rae Jepsen Has Perfect Advice for Anyone Going Through a Breakup." Insider.com, October 9, 2017.

"Exclusive GRAMMY.com Interview with Carly Rae Jepsen." Grammy.com, December 2, 2014.

Chang, Clio. "The Case for Carly Rae Jepsen." *The New Republic,* August 26, 2016.

Cragg, Michael. "Carly Rae Jepsen: 'I sound gritty because I was vaping for a week.'" *Guardian,* April 23, 2015.

Laurence, Emily. "Carly Rae Jepsen Chats with *Seventeen*!" *Seventeen,* August 27, 2012.

Savage, Mark. "How Carly Rae Jepsen Shrugged Off 'Call Me Maybe.'" BBC News, December 18, 2015.

Thompson, Eliza. "Carly Rae Jepsen: 'You Can't Write Music to Prove Something.'" *Cosmopolitan,* January 29, 2016.

Ugwu, Reggie. "What Makes Carly Rae Jepsen a Pop Star?" BuzzFeed, December 15, 2015.

Waters, Michael. "Carly Rae Jepsen's Queer Renaissance." Electric Lit, May 2, 2018.

### CELINE DION

Della Cava, Marco. "Celine Dion: Rene hopes to 'die in my arms.'" *USA Today,* August 23, 2015.

Hakim, Danny. "The Media Business: Advertising; Can Celine Dion Help Chrysler Rebound? The Automaker Is Betting Millions That She Can." *New York Times,* November 5, 2002.

Wilson, Carl. *Celine Dion's Let's Talk About Love: A Journey to the End of Taste.* New York: Bloomsbury Academic, 2017.

### CHRISTINA AGUILERA

Helligar, Jeremy. "Can Christina Aguilera Reclaim Her (Rightful) Place on the Pop Star Throne?" *Variety,* June 15, 2018.

Jones, Allie. "Christina Aguilera on 'Longing for Freedom' & Her Hip-Hop-Inspired Return to Music." *Billboard,* May 3, 2018.

## DEMI LOVATO

*Breakfast Television,* Citytv, October 19, 2015.

*Demi Lovato: Simply Complicated.* Directed by Hannah Lux Davis. Los Angeles: Philymack Productions, 2017.

Rapkin, Mickey. "Demi Lovato on Touring with DJ Khaled, Avoiding 'Fake' People & the Need for Brutal Honesty." *Billboard,* March 8, 2018.

Silverman, Amanda. "Demi Lovato: 'I Knew at a Young Age I Had a Problem.'" *Elle,* October 7, 2015.

Valby, Karen. "Demi Lovato Opens Up About Living Sober, Finding Her Voice & Feeling Confident." Refinery29, May 17, 2016.


## GWEN STEFANI

"The 25 Best Albums of 2016 (So Far)." *Entertainment Weekly,* May 26, 2016.

Ganz, Caryn. "Gwen Stefani Climbs Back from the Abyss." *New York Times,* March 10, 2016.

Nelson, Jeff. "Gwen Stefani Dishes on Her New Music: 'I Would Consider It a Breakup Record.'" *People,* November 10, 2015.

Petersen, Anne Helen. "The New Gwen Stefani Is a Lot Like the Old One." BuzzFeed, July 17, 2018.

Rainey, Candice. "The All-Star: Gwen Stefani." *Elle,* May 4, 2011.


## JANELLE MONÁE

*All Things Considered,* NPR, December 21, 2018.

Andrews, Gillian "Gus." "Janelle Monae Turns Rhythm and Blues Into Science Fiction." Gizmodo, July 21, 2010.

Empire, Kitty. "Janelle Monae: Dirty Computer Review—From Dystopian Android to R&B Party Girl." *Guardian,* April 28, 2018.

Grierson, Tim. "Why Janelle Monae's 'Dirty Computer' Film Is a Timely New Sci-Fi Masterpiece." *Rolling Stone,* April 27, 2018.

O'Connor, Roisin. "What Did We Do to Deserve Janelle Monae? *Dirty Computer*—Review." *Independent,* April 27, 2018.

Perpetua, Matthew. "Janelle Monae: *The ArchAndroid.*" Pitchfork, May 20, 2010.

Ringen, Jonathan. "How Singer-Songwriter, Actress-Activist Janelle Monae Gets So Much Done." *Fast Company,* November 19, 2018.

Spanos, Brittany. "Janelle Monae Frees Herself." *Rolling Stone,* April 26, 2018.

Vidal, Dan. "Janelle Monae—*The ArchAndroid* (Review)." URB, May 19, 2010.

Wortham, Jenna. "How Janelle Monae Found Her Voice." *New York Times Magazine,* April 19, 2018.


## JENNIFER HUDSON

Doyle, Patrick. "Jennifer Hudson Celebrates Justice Ginsburg, Female Trailblazers in 'I'll Fight' Video." *Rolling Stone,* November 14, 2018.

Greenstreet, Rosanna. "Jennifer Hudson: 'I've loved all my jobs, even when I worked at Burger King.'" *Guardian,* January 6, 2018.

Hudson, Jennifer. "Jennifer Hudson's Aha! Moment." *O, The Oprah Magazine,* October 2007.

Kelly, Guy. "Jennifer Hudson Interview: 'I wouldn't pay attention to what Simon Cowell says about vocals.'" *Telegraph,* January 7, 2017.


## JENNIFER LOPEZ

Chocano, Carina. "Jennifer Lopez Is (Still) on Top of the World." *Harper's Bazaar,* January 9, 2019.

Gardner, Elysa. "She's Got the Moves and Grooves." *Los Angeles Times,* May 30, 1999.

Kennedy, Gerrick D. "Ahead of 'American Idol' Debut, Jennifer Lopez Gets 'On the Floor' in Leaked RedOne-Produced Single." *Los Angeles Times* Pop & Hiss blog, January 17, 2011.

"On the 6." *NME,* September 12, 2005.

Van Meter, Jonathan. "Jennifer Lopez: Venus Rising." *Vogue,* March 15, 2012.


## KACEY MUSGRAVES

Caramanica, Jon. "Everyday Tales About a Tough World. But That's Life." *New York Times,* October 19, 2012.

Coscarelli, Joe. "'Slow Burn': Watch Kacey Musgraves Turn Country Music Psychedelic." *New York Times,* October 24, 2018.

Erlewine, Stephen Thomas. "Kacey Musgraves, *Golden Hour.*" AllMusic, retrieved October 1, 2019.

Feeney, Nolan. "Kacey Musgraves Details 'Trippy' New Album *Golden Hour,* Coming Early 2018." *Entertainment Weekly,* December 12, 2017.

Hight, Jewly. "Think Politics Is Gone from Country Music? Listen Closer." NPR's *The Record,* March 20, 2018.

Jenkins, Craig. "On Kacey Musgraves's *Golden Hour,* a Star Is Born." Vulture, March 30, 2018.

Weiner, Natalie. "Kacey Musgraves on Her Stunning New Album, Nashville Double Standards, and How Psychedelics Made a 'Giant Impression' on Her." *Billboard,* March 29, 2018.

## KATY PERRY

Hudson, Kathryn. "Katy Perry: Elle Canada Interview." *Elle Canada,* August 29, 2013.

"Photos: Katy Perry July Cover." *Vogue,* June 17, 2013.

Wallace, Amy. "The GQ Cover Story: Katy Perry." *GQ,* January 21, 2014.

Willman, Chris, and Shirley Halperin. "Katy Perry and Kacey Musgraves on Country-Pop Crossover, Pot, 'Songs That Take Balls to Sing' (Q&A)." *Hollywood Reporter,* May 27, 2014.

## KELLY CLARKSON

Azzopardi, Chris. "American Unbridled." *QSaltLake,* November 21, 2017.

Bueno, Antoinette. "Kelly Clarkson Hilariously Reveals the Secret to Her Recent Slim-Down." ETOnline.com, May 22, 2018.

Clements, Erin. "Kelly Clarkson Reveals Songwriting Secret, Recurring Dream for HuffPost's #nofilter." HuffPost, October 11, 2013.

Friedman, Megan. "Kelly Clarkson Says 'Wine Is Necessary' as a Mom." *Cosmopolitan,* January 10, 2018.

Ganz, Caryn. "Kelly Clarkson Is Nobody's Puppet." *New York Times,* October 19, 2017.

Johnston, Maura. "Kelly Clarkson: 'I Am a Whole Lot of Woman, and That's OK.'" *Rolling Stone,* October 26, 2017.

Kiefer, Elizabeth. "Kelly Clarkson Reveals the Sad Meaning Behind 'Piece by Piece.'" Refinery29, March 1, 2016.

Setoodeh, Ramin. "Kelly Clarkson on Her New Album, 'The Voice' and How Michelle Obama Inspired a Song." *Variety,* October 2017.

Stern, Abby, and Karen Mizoguchi. "Kelly Clarkson Says It's 'Really Crucial' to Instill Self-Esteem in Her Kids: 'Always Stand Up for Yourself.'" *People*, October 13, 2017.


KESHA

Coscarelli, Joe, and Katie Rogers. "Kesha vs. Dr. Luke: Inside Pop Music's Contentious Legal Battle." *New York Times,* February 23, 2016.

*Good Morning America.* ABC, July 31, 2018.

Hiatt, Brian. "The Liberation of Kesha." *Rolling Stone*, October 4, 2017.

Johnston, Maura. "Kesha and Dr. Luke: Everything You Need to Know to Understand the Case." *Rolling Stone,* February 22, 2016.

Kesha. "Kesha Fights Back in Her New Single, 'Praying.'" Lenny Letter, July 6, 2017.

Lorusso, Marissa. "Kesha Walks Us Through Her 'Rainbow,' Track by Track." NPR's *All Songs Considered*, August 11, 2017.

Reed, Ryan. "Read Kesha's Poignant Essay About Celebratory New Song 'Woman.'" *Rolling Stone*, July 13, 2017.

Scaggs, Austin. "Party Animal: Behind Ke$ha's Big Debut." *Rolling Stone,* January 26, 2010.

Snapes, Laura. "Kesha Returns: 'Rainbow Is Truly from the Inside of My Guts.'" *Guardian*, July 6, 2017.


LADY GAGA

Bailey, Alyssa. "Lady Gaga on the Orlando Shootings: 'This Is an Attack on Humanity Itself.'" *Elle*, June 14, 2016.

Koha, Nui Te. "Why the World Is Going GaGa." *Herald Sun*, May 16, 2009.

"Lady Gaga Opens Up About Sexual Assault and Mental Health in Vulnerable ELLE Women in Hollywood Acceptance Speech." Elle.com, October 16, 2018.

*On Air with Ryan Seacrest.* KIIS-FM Los Angeles, August 13, 2013.

Syme, Rachel. "The Shape Shifter." *New York Times Magazine*, October 3, 2018.

## LAURA JANE GRACE

Eells, Josh. "The Secret Life of Transgender Rocker Tom Gabel." *Rolling Stone*, May 31, 2012.

Feeney, Nolan. "Laura Jane Grace of Against Me!: 'I Didn't Know If the Band Was Going to Stay Together.'" *Time*, January 7, 2015.

*Fresh Air.* NPR, April 4, 2017.

Grace, Laura Jane, with Dan Ozzi. *Tranny: Confessions of Punk Rock's Most Infamous Anarchist Sellout.* New York: Hachette Books, 2016.

Ruskin, Zack. "6 Things I Learned About Against Me!'s Laura Jane Grace." *SFWeekly,* November 30, 2016.


## MARIAH CAREY

Norment, Lynn. "Mariah Carey." *Ebony,* March 1991.


## MARY J. BLIGE

"The Business of Being Ms. Mary J. Blige." Spotify for Artists, November 19, 2018.

Carter, Kelley L. "Mary J. Blige Opens Up About Her Message, Her Music and Yes—Her Marriage." The Undefeated, September 27, 2016.

Davis, Rachaell. "Mary J. Blige on How Witnessing Abuse During Childhood Shaped Her Music: 'I'd Never Seen a Woman Treated Right Other Than My Grandmother.'" *Essence,* December 22, 2018.

Escobedo Shepherd, Julianne. "Mary J. Blige: *Strength of a Woman*." Pitchfork, May 1, 2017.

Jacobs, Matthew. "How 'Mudbound' Director Dee Rees Convinced Mary J. Blige to Join Her Cast." HuffPost, November 22, 2017.

Mizoguchi, Karen. "Mary J. Blige Says 'I Didn't Know How Vain I Was' Until Going Makeup-Free for Mudbound." *Essence,* January 3, 2018.

Nicholson, Rebecca. "Mary J. Blige: 'I lost my gut and my gift. But I got it back.'" *Guardian,* November 5, 2017.

Solway, Diane. "Mary J. Blige and Carrie Mae Weems in Conversation: On Race, Women, Music and the Future." *W,* November 6, 2017.

# SOURCES

### M.I.A.

*Morning Edition.* NPR, November 5, 2013.

Phillips, Lior. "People Forget I'm Many Things: M.I.A. on Identity, Politics and Being Understood." Consequence of Sound, September 9, 2016.

### MIRANDA LAMBERT

Hendrickson, Matt. "Miranda Lambert on Why She Won't 'Take Pain for Granted' & Refusing to Write Political Songs." *Billboard,* July 27, 2017.

Jones, Maggie. "Miranda Lambert Pours Out Emotions at Knoxville Concert." *USA Today* Network, March 2, 2018.

Keeps, David A. "At Home with Miranda Lambert." *Good Housekeeping,* November 3, 2015.

Sanneh, Kelefa. "Miranda Lambert's Power Play." *The New Yorker,* November 6, 2016.

Sodomsky, Sam. "Miranda Lambert: *The Weight of These Wings.*" Pitchfork, December 6, 2016.

Yahr, Emily. "Miranda Lambert Is a Superstar. But Can She Get a No. 1 on Country Radio Only If She Sings with a Man?" *Washington Post,* November 12, 2018.

### MISSY ELLIOTT

Als, Hilton. "The New Negro." *The New Yorker,* October 20, 1997.

Davis, Rachaell. "*Essence* to Honor Missy Elliott at 2018 'Black Women in Music' Celebration." *Essence,* December 14, 2017.

"Missy Elliott Tries to Break Up Radio Monotony." MTV News, July 29, 1997.

St. Félix, Doreen. "Missy Elliott's 'Supa Dupa Fly.'" *The New Yorker*'s Touchstones.

### NICKI MINAJ

Beaudoin, Kate. "17 Times Nicki Minaj Perfectly Shut Down Sexism." Mic, April 3, 2015.

Burney, Lawrence. "7 Highlights from Nicki Minaj's Already Legendary Interview with Zane Lowe." *Vice,* April 12, 2018.

Fitzgerald, Trent. "Nicki Minaj Talks Foxy Brown + Jay-Z Inspiration, 'Pink Friday: Roman Reloaded' Goes Platinum." PopCrush, June 28, 2012.

Jefferson, J'na. "'Queen' and the Hypocrisy of Nicki Minaj's Feminism." *Vibe*, August 17, 2018.

Sandell, Laurie. "Nicki Minaj Wants All Women to Demand More Orgasms." *Cosmopolitan*, May 29, 2015.

Sieczkowski, Cavan. "Nicki Minaj Tells V Magazine, 'I Love Women Who Take Control.'" HuffPost, November 6, 2014.

*Sway in the Morning*. Sirius XM, November 26, 2013.

## PINK

Ahmed, Tufayel. "Pink on New Album 'Beautiful Trauma,' Trump and Music Industry Sexual Harassment: Trump Is 'Rock Bottom, I'm Sad and Heartbroken.'" *Newsweek*, October 13, 2017.

Blackstone, Tiffany. "Playing Mom and Rock Star: Pink Says She's 'Never Juggled So Many Damn Plates.'" *Redbook*, May 14, 2018.

Hunter-Tilney, Ludovic. "Pink Interview: From Tales of Excess to Songs About Motherhood." *Financial Times*, December 8, 2017.

Nicholson, Rebecca. "Pink: 'Monogamy is work. You have times when you haven't had sex in a year.'" *Guardian*, October 13, 2017.

"Pink's Advice for Her Daughter Willow Is the Cutest Thing You'll Hear Today." *Cosmopolitan*, December 6, 2017.

*Watch What Happens Live with Andy Cohen*. Bravo, October 19, 2017.

## QUEEN LATIFAH

*Ebro in the Morning*. Hot 97 FM, July 19, 2017.

Guerra, Julia. "Here's How Queen Latifah Stays Balanced, No Matter What Chaos Is in Her Kingdom—Exclusive." Elite Daily, February 28, 2019.

Hodari Coker, Cheo. "Queen Latifah Aims to Reign Over Films Too." *Los Angeles Times*, November 6, 1996.

Hunt, Dennis. "Queen Latifah delivers smooth, confident message." *Baltimore Sun*, December 5, 1991.

Waltrous, Peter. "When the Queen Speaks, People Listen." *New York Times*, August 25, 1991.

# SOURCES

## RIHANNA

Robinson, Lisa. "Rihanna in Cuba: The Cover Story." *Vanity Fair,* November 2015.

## SHAKIRA

Grattan, Steven. "Colombia Must Invest in Education to Have Peace, Singer Shakira Says." Reuters, November 2, 2018.

Sheeler, Jason. "*Glamour* February Cover Star, Shakira, Tells Us: 'I'm Not on Earth Just to Shake It and Shake It Endlessly.'" *Glamour,* February 2014.

Udovitch, Mim. "Q&A: Shakira." *Rolling Stone,* February 14, 2002.

## SIA

Aron, Hillel. "How Sia Saved Herself." *Rolling Stone,* August 24, 2018.

Cliff, Aimee. "Popping Off: Why Sia's Disappearing Act Is Changing the Landscape for Women in Pop." *The Fader,* July 11, 2014.

Dresdale, Andrea. "Sia Invited to Join the Motion Picture Academy; Says She Wants to Give Kids a 'Different Idea of Expression.'" ABC News Radio, June 29, 2016.

Hiatt, Brian. "Adele: Inside Her Private Life and Triumphant Return." *Rolling Stone,* November 3, 2015.

Kercher, Sophia. "How Sia's Videos and Performances Got Choreographed." Vulture, February 18, 2015.

Morin, Natalie. "Sia Just Took a Huge Step Forward for Women in Music." Mic, August 8, 2014.

Spanos, Brittany. "Sia's Reject Opus: Songwriter on Reclaiming Adele, Rihanna's Unwanted Hits." *Rolling Stone,* December 3, 2015.

## SOLANGE

Beyoncé. "Solange Brings It All Full Circle with Her Sister Beyoncé." *Interview,* January 10, 2017.

Coleman, Christina. "Solange's Performance at the Busboys and Poets 'Peace Ball' Was the Blackest Thing to See Before Trump's Inauguration." *Essence,* January 20, 2017.

Knowles, Solange. "Solange Wrote the Most Powerful Letter to Her Teenage Self." *Teen Vogue,* May 17, 2017.

Valdés, Mimi. "Solange Knowles Shows Us All What Can Happen When a Woman Finds Her Purpose." *Glamour,* October 30, 2017.

## SZA

Bruner, Raisa. "How Breakout R&B Star SZA Went from Sharing a Futon to Finding Her Voice." *Time,* July 20, 2017.

Erbentraut, Joseph. "You Probably Don't Know Rising R&B Star SZA Yet, But You Will." HuffPost, July 23, 2014.

Milazzo, Crissy. "SZA Opens Up About What Her Upcoming Album Will Sound Like." *Teen Vogue,* May 6, 2016.

Pareles, Jon. "SZA's Songs Face Desire in All Its Complications." *New York Times,* June 7, 2017.

## TAYLOR SWIFT

Aswad, Jem. "Taylor Swift Accuses DJ of 'Grabbing My Ass' in Court Testimony." *Variety,* August 10, 2017.

"Cover Preview: Taylor Swift Fights Back About Her Love Life, the Hyannis Port House—and Has Words for Tina Fey and Amy Poehler." *Vanity Fair,* March 5, 2013.

Eells, Josh. "The Reinvention of Taylor Swift." *Rolling Stone,* September 8, 2014.

PenzeyMoog, Caitlin. "The Case for Taylor Swift, Radical Champion of Self-Esteem." A.V. Club, November 21, 2014.

Swift, Taylor. "For Taylor Swift, the Future of Music Is a Love Story." *Wall Street Journal,* July 7, 2014.

Toomey, Alyssa. "Taylor Swift Talks Love: 'Never Give Anyone an Excuse to Say You're Crazy.'" *E! News,* February 4, 2014.

HarperCollins books may be purchased for educational, business,
or sales promotional use. For information, please email the Special
Markets Department at SPsales@harpercollins.com.

FIRST EDITION

Designed by Bonni Leon-Berman

Library of Congress Cataloging-in-Publication Data has been
applied for.

ISBN 978-0-06-294369-9

20 21 22 23 24   IM   10 9 8 7 6 5 4 3 2 1